A NEW LOOK
AT BLACK FAMILIES
SECOND EDITION

Charles Vert Willie
Harvard University

GENERAL HALL, INC.
Publishers
23–45 Corporal Kennedy Street
Bayside, New York 11360

This book is dedicated to my
parents and students,
who have taught me
many wonderful things.

Contents

Preface

By way of 18 case studies, this book answers the question of what it is like to be black in the United States. The stories of these families as told to our interviewers provide a window through which we can see patterns of variation in the life-style of affluent or middle-class, working-class, and poor black households.

Analysis of the way of life of black families, using the case method, is particularly effective in overcoming stereotypes. A comparison of adaptations by social class reveals both strengths and weaknesses that are associated with each status level.

This is a study of black families today and the situations in which they find themselves. It is not a study of the past, although there are brief references to history and slavery, that peculiar institution.

A unique aspect of this investigation into black family life is that it combines a descriptive analysis and a theoretical explanation of behavior patterns. The application of social theory to the study of family life reveals the specific areas of similarity and difference between minority and majority populations and enhances our understanding of race relations.

The comparative analysis of black and of white families is introduced but is not comprehensive. It relies upon the studies of blacks presented in this book and an analysis of the adaptations of white families that is found in the literature. The conclusions from this brief investigation indicate the need for a full comparison of case studies of white as well as of black households. This book presents a partial revelation of the rich material and profound insights that can be dervied from a comparative analysis by race and social class.

The case studies of black families have been accumulated a decade or more by participants in a course on The Black Family at Syracuse University and a course on Adaptation and Learning in Majority and Minority Families at the Harvard Graduate School of Education.

This is the second edition of *A New Look at Black Families*. The first edition, published in 1976, has been completely revised with 6 new case studies added, bringing the total number of cases presented to 18 — 6 affluent, 6 working-class, and 6 poor. In Part I, the introductory chapter has been revised and two chapters that review theoretical issues in race relations have been added. These chapters make a strong case for rejecting the Marxist and colonialist theories and using the perspective of situational sociology in analyzing race-related issues.

A new feature of this edition is the overview chapter in Part II that compares the way of life of blacks in the three social classes. This chapter precedes the presentation of the 18 case studies. In the first edition, the discussion of black family life beyond data presented in the case studies was limited to chapters that analyzed the poor. In Part III the chapters on "Bootstrap Upward Mobility" and "Intergenerational Problems of Poverty for Blacks and Whites" have been retained in this edition.

A new essay that analyzes the affluent has been added. In addition, the essays in Part III compare the way of life of blacks with whites among the affluent and the poor. The concluding chapter, completely revised, provides a theoretical discussion of the adaptations of blacks and of whites by social class.

The names and geographic locations of families have been disguised to protect their privacy. These are fictitious; but the ways of life of the households reported in this book — including their joys and sorrows, their hard times and good times — are vivid and real.

Acknowledged with appreciation are all families that cooperated and the students who faithfully reported their interview conversations with sympathy and sincerity. Contributions included in this book were prepared by Dennis Ashby, Karin Caruso, Beryl M. Dakers, Jill Kirschner Katz, Daniel G. Lowengard, Judy Mesinger, Nancy Martin, Kathleen Dickinson Rockwood, Edward Sloan, Donna Willey Schum, Carol Blanck Tannenhauser, Michael Rettig, Nanalee Raphael, and

Marshall T. Young, who attended Syracuse University. Additional interviews were prepared by Kristen Haggman Mitchell, Alan Haymon, Susan Kluver, William A. Mason, and Levi Moore, who attended Harvard University. Editorial assistance of high professional quality was rendered by Dorothy Sickles and Katharine Parker. The manuscript was skillfully typed by Mary Walsh, Jane Frost, and Betty Blake. My wife, Mary Sue, and our three children — Sarah Susannah, Martin Charles, and James Theodore — comforted and consoled me during the inevitable periods of frustration that are associated with attempts at creation.

Dr. Walter Broadnax, former Deputy Assistant Secretary of the Department of Health and Human Services, gave helpful administrative oversight to this project. His assistance is acknowledged with appreciation.

This project on the Black Family and Social Class was supported, in part, by a personal service contract with the Office of the Assistant Secretary for Planning and Evaluation, United States Department of Health and Human Services. However, the contents of this book do not necessarily reflect the position of that agency, and no official endorsement of these materials should be inferred.

C.V.W.
Harvard University
Cambridge, Massachusetts
August 1981

PART I

Concepts, Data, and Methods

1 INTRODUCTION

THE BLACK FAMILY IN HISTORY

The black family is still around; it has not broken down. The miracle of the black family is that it has survived and grown stronger over the years. As psychiatrist Robert Coles says, "there's sinew in the Negro family" (Coles 1965:El). It had, for one thing, to survive the family breakups resulting from the internal slave trade. It is interesting, as background for this study of conditions today, to see what Frederick Douglass, born in slavery in 1817, has to say in his autobiography.

> The reader must not expect me to say much of my family. My first experience of life, as I now remember it, ... began in the family of my grandmother and grandfather. ... The practice of separating mothers from their children and hiring them out at distances too great to admit of their meeting, save at long intervals, was a marked feature of the cruelty and barbarity of the slave system. ... It had no interest in recognizing or preserving any of the ties that bind families together or to their homes.
>
> My grandmother's five daughters [one of whom was my mother] were hired out in this way, and my only recollections of my own mother are of a few hasty visits made in the night on foot, after the daily tasks were over, and when she was under the necessity of returning in time to respond to the ... call to the field in early morning.
>
> Of my father I know nothing. Slavery had no recognition of fathers. ...
>
> Old master ... only allowed the little children to live with grandmother for a limited time; ... as soon as they were big enough they were promptly taken away. ...
>
> The time came when I must go. ... I was seven years old (Douglass 1962:27-33).

Frederick Douglass was an ingenious man. By the age of 21 years he had escaped from slavery. In disguise, he traveled from Maryland to New York and immediately sent for his fiancee, Anna Murray, who was a free woman. They were married and lived together as husband and wife 44 years until Mrs. Douglass died in 1882 (Douglass 1962:20, 204-205).

Booker T. Washington, born in slavery in 1858 or 1859, presented a similar statement of family separation. He said:

> I was born in a typical log cabin. ... In this cabin I lived with my mother and a brother and sister till after the Civil War, when we were all declared free. Of my ancestry I know almost nothing. ... I have been unsuccessful in securing any information that would throw any accurate light upon the history of my family beyond my mother. ... In the days of slavery not very much attention was given to family history and family records — that is, black family records. Of my father I know even less than of my mother, I do not even know his name. ... (Washington 1965: 15-16).
>
> My mother's husband, who was the stepfather of my brother John and myself, did not belong to the same owner as did my mother. In fact, he seldom came to our plantation. I remember seeing him there perhaps once a year, that being about Christmas time (Washington 1965:30).

Washington reported that during the war, by running away and following the federal soldiers, his stepfather found his way into the new state of West Virginia. "As soon as freedom was declared, he sent for my mother to come to the Kanawha Valley, in West Virginia. ... My stepfather had already secured a job at a salt-furnace, and he had also secured a little cabin for us to live in. ... (Washington 1965:30-31).

These excerpts from *The Life and Times of Frederick Douglass* and *Up from Slavery* by Booker T. Washington tell us two things: first, there was little opportunity for experiencing full family life among black slaves; second, former slaves were nevertheless capable of forming enduring family unions. The first fact is usually remembered; the second fact, frequently forgotten.

Some social scientists have tried to explain the higher proportion of broken families among blacks than among whites as a direct outgrowth of the slave experience. For example, Andrew Billingsley has said:

> the slave system had a crippling effect on the establishment, maintenance, and growth of normal patterns of family life among Negro people. ... This crippled the development not only of individual slaves, but of families, and hence of the

whole society of Negro people. ... The consequences these conditions wrought for Negroes under the slave system were direct and insidious. The consequences for succeeding and even modern generations of Negroes are, perhaps, less direct, but no less insidious (Billingsley 1968:68-69).

Daniel Patrick Moynihan attempts to specify the consequences: "In essence, the Negro community has been forced into a matriarchal structure which, because it is so out of line with the rest of American society seriously retards the progress of the group as a whole." He called this matriarchal structure and its alleged limitations the "fearful price" the black American community has paid "for the incredible mistreatment to which it has been subjected over the past three centuries" (U.S. Department of Labor 1965:29).

But the facts do not jibe with the assertions. The black family is not basically a matriarchal system (Jackson 1973: 186,199). Out of every 10 adult black men, 8 to 9 are in the labor force working to support their households. Moreover, 6 to 7 out of every 10 black families are two-parent households; thus, most black children grow up in households in which a mother and a father are present. The hypothesis that the slavery heritage has contributed to both a high rate of family instability and a matriarchal system fails to recognize that among intact families (the prevailing pattern) many blacks have grandparents or great-grandparents who were born as slaves. These contemporary two-parent households are stable, although some of their ancestors were not free or able to form enduring marriages.

The history of the black family in the United States must be viewed as a miraculous movement from more or less nothing to something. After slavery, black people continued to experience severe handicaps. Yet, as mentioned, 6 to 7 out of evey 10 black families in the United States are husband-wife units compared with 8 to 9 out of every 10 white families.

Because the black family has been quickly catching up in family stability (here defined as a two-parent household), it seems probable that the instability that continues is more a function of contemporary situations and circumstances than of the historic condition of slavery. For example, an indirect association has been found to exist between family income and family instability: as the family income decreases, the proportion of families headed by one parent tends to increase. Inadequate income today resulting from racial discrimination is the "fearful price" for being black and is the "incredible mistreatment" that "seriously retards the progress of the group as a whole," a fact missed by Moynihan, who tried to blame the contemporary circumstances of blacks on their group's past experiences of slavery. Poverty, racial discrimination, and family instability are linked. Poverty, of course, can be eradicated, and so can discrimination. Those interested in further stabilizing the black family could be of much help by working for the elimination of racial discrimination in employment and income. As we shall see later, more than 90 per cent of affluent black and affluent white families are two-parent households. The problem is that too few blacks are affluent.

HYPOTHESIS

Many investigators approach the study of the black family today with predetermined attitudes, often stereotyped and inflexible. They often focus on only one sector of the black population as if it were representative of the whole. Even when this error is not committed, the black family is described as a deviant adaptation from an "ideal type" — the family form that alledgedly exists among most whites.

Jerold Heiss states that "an indictment has been handed down against the black family." He states that "the key aspect of the accusation claims that blacks would be 'better off' if the differences in family form did not exist" (Heiss 1975:3). Thus many investigations are not so much concerned about discovering how black families cope as they are concerned with explaining why they are different from white families.

Such approaches overlook the significant reference groups for many blacks, groups that consist of other blacks. Sanctions, norms, and standards are generatied by these groups — these associations in black communities in which many black persons act out their roles and relationships. In daily interactions with others of their race, black family members engage in a wide range of behaviors that may have little, if anything, to do with whites. Yet the white society is a context with which blacks must contend. The following discussion indicates common forms of adaptation in black and in white families.

In his classic essay "Social Structure and Anomie," Robert Merton identified several kinds of adaptations that individuals make to social organization. Three that seem to be helpful in explaining the adaptations of different kinds of black families are *conformity, innovation,* and *rebellion.* The conformists acknowledge the legitimacy of societal goals and also accept the means that are prescribed for achieving them. The innovationists believe in the socially sanctioned goals but discover that the acceptable means for their achievement are not available and that therefore they must improvise new and novel methods. Or the innovationist may follow the socially sanctioned methods but develop new goals. The rebels reject both the societal goals and the sanctioned means for their achievement and seek to change the existing cultural and social structure rather than to accommodate efforts within this structure (Merton 1949:133,379). Rebellion accommodates a range of adaptations from passive resistance to violent rejection. The Mertonian theory of adaptation to social organization suggests that individuals in all families share and participate in a common system of values.

My hypothesis is that these values, though shared in common, are adapted to differentially by race and by social class. And thus, the participation of all families in social organization in the United States is influenced by these characteristics.

To test the Mertonian theory, I will examine that which is significant in the life of black families of different social classes, according to their own definition of significance. This means that black families in different social class positions will be analyzed not as deviants from any predetermined ideal type. Part I of this book presents theories, methods, and concepts about race and social class in our society. Using the case method, I will analyze in depth black families of different social classis in Part II. Part III is devoted to a brief comparative analysis of families by race. And the concluding chapter summarizes what has been found in this analysis and discusses further implications for research on black families.

DATA

During the past years, I have examined case studies of more than 300 black families. These have been obtained by students, using a standard schedule of questions developed by me. The families interviewed reside in northern and southern sections of the United States, although most are northern residents who migrated from the South. Household composition varies from extended, to two-parent, to one-parent units. There are small households and families with many children. The case studies have been obtained, as an assignment, by students enrolled in my courses on The Black Family and Minority and Majority Families.

An assignment that requires direct contact with families is a meaningful pedagogical technique. The responsibility for locating a family to interview was that of each student. Some interviewed families in the community of the college or university of their enrollment. Other interviewed families in their hometowns. Some interviewed families who were friends, referred to them by friends, referred by an agency, or selected by random by knocking on the door of a stranger. When possible, the interview was conducted in the home of a family.

The interview schedule requested specific information about family customs, aspirations of parents for children, and patterns of authority within the family (see Appendix A).

Interviewers were black and white undergraduate and graduate students. Out of the 300 or more case studies 18 have been selected for detailed analysis in this book as representative of three social class levels — the affluent, the working class, and the poor. There are 6 families in each of 3 social class categories. The economic resources of a family are the primary basis for assigning families to each class level. Affluent, or middle-class, families have annual family incomes at or above the national median. Working-class families have incomes that range from above the official federal poverty line up to the national median. Poor families are those below the official poverty line. Roughly, about one-third of all black families is affluent; one-third, working-class; and one-third, poor. The primary factor that determines whether or not a case study is included in this volume is the quality of the student's report in terms of descriptive data and analysis. Families have been disguised in name, occupation, and geographic area to protect their privacy.

Because blacks are often referred to in the literature as if they were a homogeneous group, 18 families of the same race but of different income levels are analyzed to determine if, in fact, their ways of life, customs, and practices are similar. This study thus has very limited goals (1) of ascertaining the presence or absence of a common way of life among black families of similar and different income levels, and (2) of determining if black families differ from white families of a similar social class. Generalizations about the frequency of certain behavior forms within the total black population is not our goal. Although I do not claim that the 18 families are representative of all blacks, their ways of life are illustrative of adaptations in different social classes.

THE INTERVIEWERS — BLACK AND WHITE

Before undertaking the interview, many black students tended to project the experiences of their home life upon other blacks and assumed that they behaved in similar ways. Stereotyping may apply to an Ingroup as well as an Outgroup. Black students especially were likely to stereotype all blacks as leading a common way of life because of their common experience of racial oppression in the United States. According to this view, the struggle against racism is all-consuming, demanding unity and commitment toward a common cause and, therefore, levels all differences among blacks. This study will determine the truthfulness or falsity of this assumption.

Initially, the black students resisted the assigment for other reasons too. They insisted that blacks had been studied too often and that no good could come from prying around in the private affairs of other black people. I held firmly to the assignment and insisted that it would enhance the students' understandings and insights. I admitted, however, that blacks have been studied often but tried to point out that seldom has the black family been observed and analyzed as an integrated and adaptive system, that most observers have considered it to be a deviant form. Thus black students were urged to carry through with the interview for the value they would derive from an intimate understanding of a family other than their own, and as a way of helping to set the record straight. Black students who continued to protest on the principle that blacks have been studied too much were given permission to inteview whites so that comparative data could be made available. After winning the freedom to interview others, most blacks were contented to interview blacks. They developed excellent case studies, as you will see, using a common interview schedule.

The white students also were reluctant to follow through with the interview. Some white students were embarrassed to ask the blacks to share intimate information with them. A few whites were annoyed with the prospect of having to beg blacks to grant them an interview. Others were fearful of calling on blacks in a black neighborhood. Many whites confessed that they did not know any blacks and did not know how to go about contacting a black family. They were worried about how they would be received. The assignment was unsettling.

Again, I held firmly to the requirements of the course. The white students had to transcend their fears. They did this in various ways and prepared case studies that were excellent. After the interview experience, the white students were ecstatic in commenting upon their new insights, which had freed them from lifetime stereotypes of the black family. They had thought of the black family as poor and disorganized. They found some black families poor and some black families disorganized. But most were stable and sound.

By and large the 18 case studies indicate that the students, though inexperienced in interviewing, awkward and naive in their approach, established honest and trusting relationships with the families and obtained basic facts and elicited information about some important feelings. Reported are the results of a guided conversation. Because all students asked similar questions of all families, the opportunity for comparative analysis is presented. I believe that the students have rendered good reports of a range of adaptations among black families in the United States.

THE FAMILIES

Too frequently in the past, the description and analysis of black family life has emphasized that which is unique, exotic, and different. The interview schedule designed for this study was for the prupose of getting at the everyday hapenings in the lives of black people. We were trying to understand a style of life, a way of life — the habits of family members, the customs and conventions of the group. Researchers had to be sensitive to the variety of life-styles among blacks and the situational determinants of different family forms and patterns of adaptation. A summary of situational difference of black families by social class follows.

Affluent black families tend to be nuclear households consisting of husband and wife and two or three children. Working-class black families tend to be nuclear households, too, consisting of husband and wife and children. However, the working-class black family is likely to be larger, with five or more children present. Also, there is the possibility that a relative or boarder may be part of the working-class household. Working-class black families are broken more often than are those that are affluent, with illness and death frequently among the reasons for the absence of the male spouse. Poor black families are likely to be one-parent households more often than are families in the other class levels. Some are extended families consisting of grandmother, mother, and children. Among the poor, desertion and divorce are chief causes for family disruption. One-parent households are not always without a male presence, however; a boyfriend may visit frequently, help support the mother, and be attentive to her children. A more detailed overview of black families by social class is presented in Part II.

All blacks — affluent, working-class, and poor — are so deeply involved in work that they seldom have much time for voluntary community activity. Nevertheless, there are some interesting variations by social class. Affluent black parents tend to be active participants in church affairs, mainstays of the Parent-Teacher Association or a school-community group, and possibly members of a social club. Black working-class parents tend to attend church worship services regularly; the mother may periodically go to meetings of the school-community group; and that is about all the family can do. Poor black families tend to be univolved in community affairs and may or may not be church members. Those who are faithful in church attendance are likely to be completely enveloped by the religious system, but many have no church affiliation and no other organized community participation. Visiting with family members and a few friends is about all that they do as a leisure-time activity outside the home.

Thus, we see different and distinct styles of life among blacks of different class levels associated with family composition, child-rearing, and community participation. A fuller discussion of these differences is presented in Part II.

These case studies should help lay to rest for all time the tendency to stereotype blacks. This study of black families by social class indicates the diversity within the race. Despite the diversity there are some common responses among families with similar resources and opportunities. This is the story of 18 families who are both similar to and different from other blacks and all families in the United States.

REFERENCES

Billingsley, Andrew, 1968. *Black Families in White America*. Englewood

Cliffs, N.J.: Prentice-Hall.

Coles, Robert. 1965. "There's Sinew in the Negro Family." Background paper for White House Conference on Civil Rights, Washington, D.C., November 1965. Reprinted from the *Washington Post*, October 10, 1965.

Douglass, Frederick. 1962. *Life and Times of Frederick Douglass.* New York: Macmillan (first published in 1892).

Heiss, Jerold. 1975. *The Case of the Black Family.* New York: Columbia University Press.

Jackson, Jacquelyn Johnson. 1973. "Black Women in a Racist Society." In *Racism and Mental Health,* edited by C.V. Willie, et. al., Pittsburgh: University of Pittsburgh Press.

Merton, Robert K. 1949. *Social Structure and Social Theory.* New York: Free Press.

U.S. Department of Labor. 1965. *The Negro Family.* Washington, D.C.: U.S. Government Printing Office.

Washington, Booker T. 1965. *Up From Slavery.* New York: Dell.

Chapter 2 THEORIES OF THE ADAPTATION OF BLACKS IN AMERICAN SOCIETY

MARXIST AND COLONIALIST THEORIES

Of the more popular theoretical explanations of race relations in the United States, the Marxist explanation of labor exploitation and the colonialist thesis have gained much attention. The Marxists contend that capitalists created slavery or semi-slavery as a system of cheap labor and as a way of subduing potential white competitors by splitting the labor force along racial lines. The colonialists classify ghettoes or contained communities of blacks and other racial minorities as colonies that are deliberately left underdeveloped and that are dominated socially, politically, and economically by outsiders or whites. The school, an important institution in black and other communities, is described by Samuel Bowles and Herbert Gintis as "foster[ing] types of personal development compatible with the relationship of dominance and subdominance in the economic sphere" (Bowles and Gintis 1976:11).

As evidence that the alleged conspiracy of white capitalists has worked, white workers are described as not being allies of the black revolution but indeed enemies of it (Boggs 1969: 54-55). To indicate how black ghettoes are under outside control, Joseph Lohman has stated that minority groups view the law as not of their making and not in their interest, but as a foreign power. Moreover, he said that they view the police as an army of occupation (Altschuler 1970:41).

There are several difficulties with these theoretical perspectives for analyzing the black community. First, they do not account for variations within the black population. In Stephen Birmingham's book *Certain People,* the life-styles of several

16

black millionaires are described (Birmingham 1977). These individuals have prospered by developing products and services especially for but not limited to the black community. They, therefore, are not part of a white capitalist conspiracy to perpetuate cheap labor. Indeed, these blacks have prospered because other blacks have prospered.

Also there is evidence that less affluent blacks and less affluent whites have united in common cause more frequently than have more affluent blacks and more affluent whites. For example, blue-collar white workers and blacks have teamed up often, but not always, in presidential elections (Newman 1978:17-31). Specifically, Dorothy Newman and her associates point out that "the greatest power blacks have over public policy is in their numbers in places where, from lack of choice in housing or neighborhoods, they make up a majority or an important swing vote in the electorate."

Thomas Pettigrew reminds us that "the American racial scene has always been highly complex, varied, and inconsistent, defying facile generalizations." He points out that some white workers may oppose school desegregation and yet never think of the interracial neighborhood in which they live as strange or unusual (Pettigrew 1971:264). Only recently has the residential integration of affluent blacks with affluent whites begun to catch up with that which has characterized lower-income blacks and lower-income whites in the past (Simkus 1978: 81-93). Karl and Alma Taeuber report that economic differentials such as occupational rank have diminished between the races but that "residential segregation persists." In fact, they conclude that "it is implausible to attribute the high degrees of residential segregation of Negroes from whites to differences in the ... value of the homes they own." This conclusion led them to predict that "improving the economic status of Negroes is unlikely by itself to alter prevailing patterns of racial residential segregation" (Taeuber and Taeuber 1969:94-95). The studies of blacks in cities by these researchers reveal clear and present evidence of resistance of affluent whites to accepting affluent blacks in their neighborhoods.

The school desegregation effort in Corpus Christi, Texas

raises serious questions about the alleged antagonism between the working class of different races because of their competition for scarce jobs. Already it has been shown that less separation exists between working-class blacks and whites in residential neighborhoods than between the affluent of both races. In Corpus Christi, expenses for litigating the school desegregation case that created great racial tension were paid for by an organization that represents working-class people of different races — the United Steel Workers of America, a labor union (Cirilo-Medina and Purdy 1981:140). It is not possible to explain such happenings as these by Marxist principles. In higher-income levels where resources are plentiful and there is allegedly less competition between the races, there is more separation. In lower-income levels where there are scarce resources and allegedly more competition between the races, there is relatively more cooperation and desegregation.

The Marxist perspective, which treats social differentiation and discrimination by race as an economic variable, fails to explain why there is greater segregation between the affluent of different races than between the working-class or poor people of different races. Also Marxist principles do not explain why white capitalists give the white poor with limited education better paying jobs than the black poor who are similarly educated. Because numerically there are more poor whites than poor blacks (they outnumber blacks three to one), the capitalists, in terms of Marxist ideology, ought to have favored black workers over white workers, if race relations were economic in origin — so that the former could be coerced to conform because of the larger pool of available cheap white labor that could displace nonconforming blacks. But clearly, the white poor have been favored over the black poor in capitalistic America. Some factor other than the economics of the situation is operating. Some people call that factor racism.

The colonialist perspective also has limitations, one of which is that it treats racial minorities as if their way of life was totally dominated by the majority. It is doubtful that any group can fully dominate the social life of another group. All ghetto-ized populations everywhere have maintained their folk beliefs and values despite external pressure to conform to the dominant group. These beliefs and values sustain the subdominant group and enable its members to endure. The spirituals, for example, emerged out of a common experience of black folk that no dominant group could suppress. The major limitation of the colonialist perspective is that it does not acknowledge the inevitable interdependency that develops between two populations that share a common setting. When two groups coexist in the same area, their fates become intertwined (whether or not they acknowledge it) so much so that one group cannot destroy the other without ultimately destroying itself.

The proponents of the colonialist theory emphasize the exploitation of the subdominant group by the dominant group and tend to ignore the veto power of subdominants over the dominants and ultimately over the whole society. The colonialist theory is an appropriate explanation of the relationships between dominant and subdominant racial populations only when the two groups do not share a common area.

SITUATIONAL ANALYSIS

Twentieth-century Nazi Germany is evidence that the fate of dominant and subdominant racial or ethnic populations that occupy a common territory is intertwined. When Nazi Germans tried to destroy Jewish people who dwelt among them, they contributed ultimately to the destruction of the German nation, which is now divided into two separate countries.

The veto power of subdominants has not been a popular theme of analysis among social scientists of the colonialist orientation, whose theory of race relations has focused largely on the strategies of control by the dominants. Although the Marxist social scientists have paid more attention to the subdominants than have the colonialists, their race-relations theory is defective in that it does not explain the absence of oppressive practices toward the black working class by affluent blacks, and the presence of cooperative behavior between some members of both the black and the white working classes despite the scarce resources available to these groups. Another defect of these two theoretical explanations is that they portray subdominants always as passive, reacting to the initiatives of others. This, of course, is an inappropriate characterization. Finally, they erroneously describe subdominants as people without choice.

Rather than rely upon global theories that contribute to stereotypes or distorted pictures, a more appropriate analysis of blacks in American society, and particularly black families, might flow from situational sociology, which assumes that the behavior of most people is structured by particular situations. This assumption may be extended to include race relations that tend to be shaped, according to Pettigrew, by "specific situational norms" (Pettigrew 1971:264-265).

"In order to comprehend some of the complexity of American racial patterns," Pettigrew said, "it becomes necessary to examine separately some of the major institutions of American society" (Pettigrew 1971:267). This book analyzes the specific situational norms that guide and govern the behavior of affluent, working-class, and poor black families. A particular benefit of situational analysis is that it protects against the tendency to project findings pertaining to the adaptation of one group that experiences a certain set of circumstances upon another group whose circumstances may be different. Also it helps overcome ethnocentric interpretations.

In situational analysis, all social relationships in human society are matters of choice, and all human beings are free to seek a set of relationships different from those that exist. Moreover, a different set of relationships is possible theoretically in each new situation despite the pattern of social interaction that existed between the participants of a system in the past. For example, people in subdominant positions of power in a social system may be oppressed but they can choose not to cooperate in their own oppression. They can rebel. Rebellion is the exercise of veto power, an ever present option even in coercive systems.

The act of rebellion is a choice, as is the decision to abide by the requirements of a coercive system. Choice, of course, is an action that is possible only by one who essentially is free.

Even in a system of coercion, the freedom of each participant is ever present, the freedom to participate or not to participate in such a system and, of course, to experience the negative or positive consequences of such action.

Individuals in human society arrive at definitions of their situations and determine appropriate action in terms of their self-interest. Self-interest is the fundamental basis of decisions and choices. One can determine why a system is organized as it is by determining which individuals are in charge and what is their self-interest. Thus, change in a social system primarily is a function of change in the definition of self-interest by the participants. Neither change nor stability is taken for granted in situational sociology; each is a function of human decision in a given situation.

Self-interest is not the same as selfishness. Selfishness is the act of seeking one's own good at the expense of others. Total selfishness, of course, ultimately is a logical impossibility, for none can continue to exist without the goodwill of some who will guarantee one's safety and security. Safety and security cannot be self-determined completely. Thus, one can be selfish in some but not all human situations if one expects to survive. Self-interest is seeking one's own good by seeking that which is good for others on whom one is dependent and with whom one must interact. The fulfillment of self-interest appears to be paradoxical but in essence is a complex activity of complementarity. One obtains and maintains the benefits of social organization for oneself by finding ways of sharing the opportunities and obligations of social organization with others. Self-interest is prudent and calculating. In its purest form, self-interest is manifested in a double victory in which one fulfills oneself by fulfilling another, resulting in mutual enhancement.

Self-interest is emphasized in situational sociology because social organization is effected through individuals, and individuals have their being through social systems. "There is neither the loss of oneself by participation ... [nor] the loss of one's [society] by individualization" (Tillich 1959:187). Both the self and society are taken seriously in situational sociology.

Situational analysis, then, is based on the premise that action is tailored to fit objective circumstances — the situation (Fletcher 1966:14). Situational sociology is an attempt to describe social systems in terms of attitudes, behavior, and social settings. Situational sociology involves the construction of social system models that explain discontinuities as well as continuities in the process of human interaction and asymmetries as well as symmetries in the structure of social relations. In situational sociology, all kinds of exchange relationships are examined as real.

A study of the American black family from the perspective of situational sociology is a study of power relationships between majority and minority populations. Power is the capacity to influence others to behave in a prescribed way; it is derived either from the prerogatives of one's nominal postion or the rank of one's graduated position in society, or from a combination of both. Thus, power may be a function of the independent and joint effects of prestige and privilege (Blau 1977:31).

Privilege or authority has to do with prerogatives within a group or parameter. Conceptually, these may be dichotomized into responsibilities and obligations that are interdependent but mutually exclusive. A symbiotic relationship exists between those who are responsible for and obligated to each other. The nominal parameter is castelike, with the various ascriptive groups such as age, sex, and race coexisting along the horizontal axis. However, none of the positions within these groups — majority or minority, male or female, older or younger — is more or less significant in the viability of the social system. Responsibility and obligation are linked and both are essential; one without the other is incomplete. In other words, a majority needs a minority, males need females, and older people need younger people. Dominant people cannot go it alone without help and assistance from subdominants. These ascriptive characteristics, conceptually, are arrayed side by side because there is no intrinsic basis for classifying race, sex, age, or any other ascriptive characteristic as being more or less valuable.

Prestige and esteem exist in a continuous range of multiple ranks within a group or parameter, arrayed along the vertical axis. The parameter is classlike because of the continuous range of differentiated ranks within it. These ranks are higher or lower or they consist of more or less of something such as income, occupation, or education. That which is higher obviously is related to that which is lower, and so is that which is more related to that which is less. One category cannot exist without the other. In a society of limited resources, some people have more only because other people have less. High and low, more or less are inextricably linked and in a symbiotic way.

The achievement of prestige and esteem by some individuals over against others in society because of their education, occupation, or wealth need not be detrimental in a just society. Rawls states that "The social system is not an unchangeable order beyond human control but a pattern of human action. In justice as fairness [people] agree to share one another's fate." From the standpoint of common sense, Rawls has said, the benefits of one individual should contribute to the welfare of others (Rawls 1971:102-104).

There are four forms of justice in a properly functioning human society: commutative or one-to-one, distributive or many-to-one, contributive or one-to-many, and corporative or many-to-many (Fletcher 1966:90). When these forms of justice are implemented according to requirements of the situation, they can affect populations and social relationships of the vertical and horizontal dimensions of the social system to such an extent that all accept and fulfill their obligations and responsibilities, or give to and receive from each other in ways that are fair.

There is social pathology when a society responds to a nominal parameter as if it were a graduated parameter and a graduated parameter as if it were a nominal parameter. This is precisely what has happened in our contemporary society. People of low-education, low-occupation, and low-income rank are accommodated by the society at large as if their levels of achievement in these graduated parameters were an unchangeable function of ascription. Poor whites, members of the majority race, have been led to believe that their low estate is ascriptive or is due to the presence of racial minorities, also an ascriptive group, when in essence their problem is due to a blocked opportunity system in the graduated parameter and an unjust distribution of resources. Thus their circumstances and conditions of life are inappropriately described as intractable and are attributed to structural deficits.

People of racial minority, of female, and of younger-age status are treated sometimes as invisible groups, as persons for whom the racial majority, men, and the older age group of the nominal parameter have no responsibility. To further complicate the situation, these nominal groups are sometimes identified as part of the vertical dimension of the social system. When these misidentifications are accepted, individuals such as those in black families who experience oppression attempt to overcome it by becoming high achievers — a prescription that is appropriate for oppression in a graduated parameter but not in a nominal parameter.

What, then, is the outcome when such conceptual distortion of social organization as that described becomes conventional wisdom? The adaptations of some whites who are poor and of some blacks who are affluent are two good illustrations of the negative consequences of accepting a distorted view of social organization that treats a nominal variable as if it were a graduated variable, and vice versa.

Comparative studies of family life reveal that some poor whites are alienated from society, more alienated than some blacks, and adapt to others in an apathetic and fatalistic way. And some affluent blacks are high-achieving conformists, more conformists than whites, whose adaptation to others is filled with anxiety as they aggressively pursue the goal of excellence — trying to be better, trying to be the best. These facts may contribute to the experience of poor whites who tend to score higher on alienation scales than other groups (Brink and Harris 1961:135), and of blacks who tend to have a higher rate of hypertension than other groups.

Those who wish to exploit poor whites do not encourage them to view their station in life as a function of the vertical dimension of society in which the rich and the poor are functionally interrelated. Believing their poverty to be fully a function of family of birth, which is a nominal variable, poor whites

Chapter **3** THE CONTINUING
SIGNIFICANCE OF RACE

In some respects William Wilson can be called the god-father of this discussion on the continuing significance of race. He wrote a book, *The Declining Significance of Race,* which immediately caught the attention of the white press in the United States. The *New York Times* and the *Washington Post* carried multiple news stories of his book.

At the same time that the popular press lavished attention upon the Wilson work, and professional journals provided extensive space for commentaries, other important contemporary studies about race relations in the United States received only limited attention. Such was the study prepared by Dorothy Newman and colleagues entitled *Protest, Politics, and Prosperity* and subtitled "Black Americans and White Institutions, 1940-75."

Richard Margolis, literary editor of *Change* magazine, states that "in the war of reviews Wilson has won hands down. ... even the *New York Times,* not the world's most roseate journal, considers Wilson's sophisticated optimism more convincing than Newman's straightforward gloom" (Margolis 1979:106). Margolis tries to interpret why reviewers have preferred Wilson's bright mirage to Newman's dark mirror. He states that "it may be because they ... are weary of domestic strife and guilt-edged sermons." These days, he states, "many Americans are ... eager to accept glad racial tidings with no questions asked, especially when they come to us courtesy of a brilliant black scholar ..." (Margolis 1979:106-107).

Wilson acknowledges that "the presence of blacks is still firmly resisted in various institutions and social arrangements, for example, in residential areas and private social clubs." But with reference to jobs, he states that "talented and educated blacks are experiencing unprecedented job opportunities in the

27

growing government and corporate sectors." He claims that talented and educated blacks are experiencing job opportunities "at a rate comparable to or, in some situations, exceeding that of whites with equivalent qualifications."

Of the black poor, Wilson states that it is their limited education rather than racial discrimination that accounts for their disadvantaged condition. Wilson sees the alleged un-precedented opportunities for affluent or middle-class blacks and the limitations of poor or inner-city blacks as clear and pre-sent evidence that "economic class is now a more important fac-tor than race in determining job placement" (Wilson 1978: 99-121).

This discussion of the continuing significance of race begins with a statement of social practice reported in newspapers rather than with a series of propositions derived from sociology studies. There is no suggestion in this approach that the methods of journalism and sociology are the same. Yet sociologists ought to seriously take into consideration what is happening around them in the formulation of their principles and propositions. A careful and critical reading of what is cur-rently happening to black and brown populations in this coun-try might have caused William Wilson to be more cautious in his conclusions.

Race relations is a continuous reminder in the United States of the requirements of the Constitution. It is one of the best indicators of how near this nation has come and how far it has failed to fulfill the basic commitment of justice for all. If this thesis is correct, then race relations in the United States is a prime indicator of the viability of this society as a democracy. Rather than declining in significance, race as such an indicator is of continuing significance.

This does not mean that, psychologically, there are not at-tempts to repress race as an indicator of the strength or weakness of our social system. The optimistic assessments about the achevement of racial minorities in the United States that are readily accepted and uncritically adopted by the majori-ty or the dominant people of power is, in effect, an attempt to repress our failures in race relations. Optimistic assessments are used as antidotes against feelings of guilt regarding our failures.

Repression prevents the development of guilt that could mobilize the nation to do better. In race relations, denial is a common way of dealing with guilt. It has been said that "a guilty conscience is the seasoning of our daily life" (Tournier 1962:10). Guilt is so difficult to deal with once it is acknowledged that the dominant people of power often attempt to put into the minds of the weak the guilt that is their own (Tournier 1962:14).

Failure to fulfill the requirements of our common codes such as those contained in the Constitution is certainly a basis for guilt. Race relations is one area in which our failure is clearly manifested. Therefore, race relations in the United States is the source of much guilt for the majority. When the burden of guilt is great, the circumstances that contribute to the guilt must be changed or else the guilt has to be denied. Thus, optimistic assessments of race relations are welcome relief for those who are carrying a heavy burden of guilt.

A recent editorial in the *Dallas Morning News* attests to the fact that racism or racist behavior has the potential to evoke much guilt among members of the majority. The techniques used by the editors of that paper to reduce the guilt were denial and a proposal for suppression. They deny that outright racial hatred exists now except perhaps among "Klansmen and unrepentant Black Panthers" and declare that racism really was a phenomenon of the 1930s when Nazis hated Jews, and maybe of the 1960s during the civil rights movement in this country. Specifically, the *Dallas Morning News* editorial states that "there are few racists in the full-blown 1930s or even 1960s sense. But there are many Americans who every day are smeared all over with the imputation of racial hostility just because they differ with self-anointed spokesmen for other races." The newspaper implied that the smear was unfair and that the terms racism or racist abused those whose behavior was so classified. Having declared that "it would be hard, in point of fact, to prove that in the United States anything like outright racial hatred persists" (this is the technique of denial), the *Dallas Morning News* concluded that the terms racism and racist are stale and weary and should be retired from our language (this is the technique of suppression).

The newspaper editorial acknowledged that there may be members of the white majority who are insensitive to racial minority aspirations, who support reduced federal spending programs that benefit minorities, or who believe that there is nothing wrong with intelligence tests because minorities may score lower on them than do whites. However, the paper believes that to hate a person because of his or her race is "a bad thing" but to deny a person "this or that favor" is something else and should not be classified as racism or racist behavior. The alleged negative behavior of some whites toward blacks, in the opinion of the *Dallas Morning News,* should be labeled by another word other than racism or racist (*Dallas Morning News,* 9/23/79).

While the editors of a major newspaper in Dallas were declaring that the terms racism and racist now "cease to mean anything in particular," black women in the same city were bringing a suit against the prestigious Republican National Bank of Dallas charging discrimination. Even before the *Dallas Morning News* editorial was written, Judge Patrick Higginbotham of the Federal District Court in Dallas ruled that "the plaintiffs have demonstrated at least *prima facie* evidence that [the Republican National Bank's] personnel practices have been infested to the core by racial and sex discrimination." For example, blacks in 1969 constituted 7.56 percent of the bank's work force but only 0.34 percent of its managers. "What makes this case so complicated," said one of the attorneys representing the plaintiffs, "is that it involves white-collar workers." The particular charges against this giant banking industry in a city where "outright racial hatred"does not persist, according to its morning newspaper, are interesting. One black woman, a college graduate, claims that she was not accepted in the bank's management trainee program to which she had applied; and another black woman alleged that she was dismissed as a clerical employee because she had married a white man. The *New York Times* reports that "the bank has prepared a massive amount of documentation to contest the charges and plans to call on its personnel officers, labor market analysts, sociologists, and statistical experts to back up its contention that it has not been remiss in its hiring and promotion of qualified blacks and women" (*New York Times* 11/5/79).

This case is clinical evidence that race continues to be significant as the alleged basis for denying opportunities to people who are not white. Moreover, the opportunities allegedly denied are in the private economic sector at the managerial and clerical level, where the applicants are not individuals with limited education.

In the governmental sector, where we have been told that talented minorities also are getting good jobs at an unprecedented rate (Wilson 1978), it is interesting to note the continuing effect of race. The election of Richard Arrington, Jr. as mayor of Birmingham, Alabama in 1979 was hailed as proof that that city had made significant racial progress. Arrington, who is black, defeated Frank Parsons, a white lawyer. But Arrington's victory was due to voting that was sharply divided along racial lines. According to the *Boston Globe,* "45 percent of the voters of Birmingham are black and 77 percent of them voted almost all of them for Arrington. Only 66 percent of the white voters turned out and [only] 10 percent of them also voted for Arrington. Arrington took 52 percent of the vote" (*Boston Globe* 11/2/79).

An editorial in the *Boston Globe,* hailing the election of a black mayor, cautioned that the public should not be "misled into thinking that Birmingham is a city where there is no racialism." Indeed, Arrington's decision to seek election was due to the refusal of the incumbent mayor to fire a white police officer who had shot and killed an unarmed black woman. And as stated earlier, the voting was sharply divided along racial lines, with a majority of white voters casting their ballots for the white candidate and a majority of blacks voting for the black candidate (*Boston Globe* 11/2/79).

Even though an editorial in the *Boston Globe* attributes the nonviolent way that executive authority in city government in Birmingham was transferred from whites to blacks as resulting from "white and black moderates working together," the facts reveal that only 10 percent of the whites voted for the first black mayor of that city; 90 percent preferred the white candidate (*Boston Globe* 11/2/79). This fact means that power tends to concede authority only when forced to do so. Thus whites in the United States tend to transfer political authority to black and brown populations only when their own numbers dwindle, when those of opposing groups increase, or when they lose control over coercive institutions such as the police department and the court. Birmingham elected its first black mayor only after blacks had increased to 45 percent of the voting population.

Lee Sloan and Robert French, who prepared a case study entitled "Black Rule in the Urban South?" state that "holding the line against black power seems to be a growing problem for metropolitan white America." They state that "it is becoming increasingly evident that whites moving out may be forfeiting political control to the blacks who are left behind." Whites attempt to regain control, according to Sloan and French, by "redefining political boundaries so that the proportion of blacks within the new political unit is decreased drastically." They say that this method of regaining control "can assume the forms of gerrymandering or annexation." Also, they classify the at-large election as another way of retaining control as numbers of a majority population began to dwindle (Sloan and French, 1977: 200).

Certainly the Houston experience is an illustration of the function of at-large elections in race relations in maintaining control by the dominants. The *New York Times* reported that "during Houston's quarter-century rise to national stature as the country's fifth largest city, its spectacular expansion has essentially been managed — or mismanaged, say a growing army of critics — by a network of businessmen and developers ... dissenters have had little voice in all this, least of all the blacks and Mexican Americans." As a result of pressure from the U.S. Justice Department, the city has agreed to a new voting arrangement by districts and at-large that will put minority representatives on the city council and thereby alter its governmental power structure. The *New York Times* states that "under the old system, all members of the Council were elected at large, which diluted the voting strength of blacks and Mexican Americans." Under the old system, "the minorities, who make up 40 to 45 persent of the city's population, have had only one representative on the City Council." Under the new arrangement, five of the 14 Council members are elected at-large and the others are chosen from each of nine geographical districts. The election by single-member districts guarantees that three or four black or Hispanic candidates are elected (*New York Times* 11/1/79).

Assessing the effect of election by single-member districts upon the Houston City Council as a decision-making authority, the *New York Times* states that this could alter "the city's very direction" in that "the Council members elected from the districts are likely to be more independent ... simply because the new structure makes them more beholden to the immediate desires of constituents in their districts and less beholden to what is loosely called 'the establishment' " (*New York Times* 11/1/79).

The Justice Department moved against the at-large election system of Houston and other big cities in Texas on the basis of authority granted to it under amendments of the Voting Rights Act of 1965 to review certain local election systems.

The past decisions of whites to move from city to suburban communities have strengthened the capacity of black and of brown populations to control city governments. Were these populations not contained within the city because of housing discrimination, their numbers would not be large enough to wrest control from whites. Thus housing discrimination, which has contributed to racial concentration, has strengthened the capacity of racial minorities to influence the public policies of cities in this nation.

On the basis of press reports, we know that inadequate education is not the basis for discrimination against black and brown populations in the United States, that racism is at the core of the rejection process. Let us take police departments and the courts as examples. Boston, Cincinnati, and New York are under court order to increase the number of minorities. High-level educational attainment is not required of police. In all cities mentioned, a charge of racial discrimination in the recruitment and promotion of police officers was made. Of the 269 sergeants on the Boston police force in July 1980, one was black, and two other blacks with permanent sergeant ratings served in higher noncivil-service posts. Moreover, there were no black lieutenants or captains. About 5 percent of the force on 1980 was black, according to a consent decree filed in the Federal District Court (*Boston Globe* 7/10/80).

Cincinnati had a police force that consisted of only a few blacks and was charged with violating the Civil Rights Act of 1964 and other federal statutes. The Justice Department charged that the Police Department of Cincinnati "had failed or refused to recruit, hire, promote and assign blacks and women on the same basis as white men and had used written tests that excluded blacks and women. According to a consent decree filed in a Federal District Court, Cincinnati promised to fill one-third of police officer vacancies with blacks and one-fourth of the openings for specialists and sergeants with blacks and women in terms of their numbers on the 1980 police recruitment list or in the pool of eligible employees," according to the *New York Times* (7/9/80).

The Executive Director of the New York Civil Liberties Union states that "the New York City Police Department ... [in 1980] has one of the lowest percentages of minority officers of any major city. ... At issue is a test which in effect screens out members of minority groups but which has never been shown to be an accurate predictor of an applicant's job performance." The city would not sign a consent decree as an indication of its commitment to the goal of equal opportunity and had to be forced by a court order of the United States Court of Appeals to hire one minority police officer for every two white officers hired (*New York Times* 7/15/80). The initial response of the mayor of New York City to the court order was to postpone hiring, pending the outcome of a legal appeal. The mayor also criticized another court ruling that sanctioned as lawful a federal public works program that reserves 10 percent of such projects for minority contractors. At first, he declared that he would not "give in" to the court order regarding police hiring.

Finally, the courts, which have been the principal means through which racial minorities and women have secured constitutional rights, have been found wanting in their own employment practices. According to one press bulletin, "data supplied ... by Federal courts confirm accusations that for the most part the courts provide only lowly jobs for women and members of minorities." Representative Don Edwards states that information compiled for the House of Representatives Subcommittee on Civil and Constitutional Rights shows "that with few exceptions employment practices in the Federal judiciary have excluded minorities and women in all but clerical and secretarial positions." According to United Press International, Federal District Court Judge Elmo B. Hunter of Missouri, testifying on behalf of the Judicial Conference of the United States, acknowledged that the allegations were "more accurate than inaccurate" (*New York Times* 6/1/80).

With the courts exhibiting ambivalence in acknowledging their full guilt with reference to minority hiring, one can understand how this nation has been flooded with a series of crazy mixed-up court-ordered school desegregation plans that have tended to grant more desegregation relief to whites who in most instances were against desegregation and have left most blacks, the plaintiffs who won the cases seeking desegregation relief, in segregated, racially isolated schools. The school desegregation plan initially ordered by a Federal District Court in Dallas left two-thirds of the black students in segregated, racially isolated schools; and the plan initially ordered by a Federal District Court in St. Louis left three-fourths of the black students in segregated, racially isolated schools. In both cities more whites than blacks experienced the benefits of school desegregation, according to the court-ordered plans. The reason for this bizarre turn of events was the assumption, sometimes implicit, sometimes explicit, on which the plans were based — that whites ought to always be the majority in desegregated schools that provide a quality education. In instances where whites were only half or less than half of the schoolwide population, too few were available to desegregate predominantly black schools if whites always had to be the majority. Whether or not there is an association between some of the inappropriate assumptions on which some court-ordered school desegregation plans are based and the miniscule number of racial minority persons employed by federal courts in professional capacities is worthy of investigation.

Up to this point, a number of cases or illustrations have been provided. The weight of evidence certainly would cause one to question a proposition that asserts that race is declining in significance. But clinical evidence does not command the respect of more systematically gathered data that uses the methodologies of the social sciences.

Based on a sample of 15,170 in a large nondecennial survey conducted in 1976, the U.S. Civil Rights Commission found that when all things were equal, including age, sex, occupation, and other characteristics, black and other minority males received an annual income that was 15 to 20 percentage points less than that received by white men (Civil Rights Commision 1978: 53-54). There is no ethical or just reason why black people should receive 15 to 20 percent less income than whites. I call this income discrepancy an unfair tax that qualified minorities pay for not being white. It is a racist tax that is withheld from their annual earnings and consequently is a form of institutional racism. In an evaluation study commissioned by the Rockefeller Foundation that involved a small sample of blacks and whites in all geographic regions who were matched by age, sex, and broad occupational categories at professional and managerial levels, I obtained a result that was similar to the finding of the Civil Rights Commission. The black and brown professional and managerial individuals in my small sample study received a median annual income that was 15 percentage points less than the median annual income for whites (Willie 1980). Indeed, I found that educated blacks had to obtain doctoral degrees to get jobs that were similar to those that some whites obtained with only a college education or a master's degree. But even after occupational parity had been achieved because of their extraordinary education, blacks lagged behind whites with similar jobs in the income they received.

The report, *All Our Children,* by the Carnegie Council

presents data by race and income analyzed by Rhona Pavis, who found that "90 percent of the income gap between blacks and whites is the result ... of lower pay for blacks with comparable levels of education and experience" (Keniston 1977:92).

I do not know the basis for this conclusion and decided to make some calculations of my own based on data presented in the Current Population Reports (U.S. Census Bureau 1978). My goal was to determine how much of the total income difference between whites and blacks or other minorities was due to the presence of racial discrimination and the absence of effective affirmative action practices to overcome such discrimination.

By keeping the analysis at the macrosocial level and by determining what had happened to the total population of blacks and other minorities of the race parameter, I obtained these results based on the assumptions that (1) black and other minority household heads should be randomly distributed throughout all ocupations so that their percentage in any particular category is the same as their percentage in the total population of the employed; (2) the median annual income is a representative figure for each household; and (3) blacks and other racial minorities ought to receive the same median income that whites receive.

On the basis of these assumptions, my calculations revealed in Table 1 that the 4.1 million households that were headed by blacks who were employed for some period of time in 1976 should have received $67.3 billion in annual income rather than $49.7 billion. In 1976, according to my calculations, racial discrimination cost employed blacks and other racial minorities $17.6 billion.

One reason blacks were $17.6 billion down from what they should have received, as shown in Table 1c, is because affirmative action had not overcome the selective employment practices by race that characterizes American society. In the high-paying professional, managerial, sales, and skilled-craft jobs, there were only 1.1 million racial minorities when there should have been 2.3 million if there had been equity in employment.

TABLE 1

Number and Income of Black and of White Workers for Longest Job Held by Household Head, U.S.A., 1976

Table 1a

Occupation	Number		Median Income	
	Black	White	Black	White
Professional, Technical, and Kindred Workers	345	6,191	$17,286	$21,925
Managers and Administrators	218	6,677	17,397	21,550
Sales Workers	86	2,557	13,706	18,681
Clerical and Kindred Workers	452	3,160	11,079	15,470
Craft and Kindred Workers	484	8,682	15,211	17,302
Operatives	1,075	6,837	13,164	14,688
Laborers	389	1,679	11,413	13,208
Farm Workers	126	1,609	4,765	12,685
Service Workers	881	2,929	8,284	12,374
Total or Median	4,056	20,321	$12,199	$17,228

Table 1b

Occupation	Number of Blacks		
	Without Affirmative Action	With Affirmative Action	Difference
Profesional, Technical, and Kindred Workers	345	588	+ 243
Managers and Administrators	218	621	+ 403
Sales Workers	86	238	− 152
Clerical and Kindred Workers	452	325	− 127
Craft and Kindred Workers	484	825	+ 341
Operatives	1,075	712	− 363
Laborers	389	186	− 203
Farm Workers	126	156	+ 30
Service Workers	881	343	− 538

TABLE 1 (cont.)

Table 1c

| | Total Income of Blacks | | | |
Occupation	(a) Inequitable Number and Median[a]	(b) Inequitable Number but Equitable Median[b]	(c) Equitable Number and Equitable Median[c]	(a)/(c) Difference[d]
Professional and Technical Workers	$ 5,963,670,000	$ 7,564,125,000	$12,891,900,000	− $6,928,230,000
Managers and Administrators	3,792,546,000	4,697,900,000	13,382,550,000	− 9,590,004,000
Sales Workers	1,178,716,000	1,606,566,000	4,446,078,000	− 3,267,362,000
Clerical and Kindred Workers	5,007,708,000	6,993,344,000	5,028,400,000	− 20,692,000
Craft and Kindred Workers	7,362,124,000	8,374,168,000	14,274,150,000	− 6,912,026,000
Operatives	14,151,300,000	15,789,600,000	10,457,856,000	+ 3,693,444,000
Laborers	4,439,657,000	5,137,912,000	2,456,688,000	+ 1,982,969,000
Farm Workers	600,390,000	1,598,310,000	197,808,000	+ 402,582,000
Service Workers	7,298,204,000	10,901,494,000	4,244,282,000	+ 3,053,922,000
Total	$49,794,315,000	$62,663,419,000	$67,379,712,000	− $17,585,397,000

a. Existing number of black workers X median income of blacks in occupational group.
b. Existing number of black workers X median income of whites in occupational group.
c. Number of black workers in occupational group is the same as proportion in total labor force nationwide and median income is the same as that for whites in occupational group.
d. The income that black workers would receive under condition of equity or effective affirmative action.
Source of data for Table la: Bureau of the Census, *Money Income in 1976 of Family and Persons in the United States* (Current Population Reports, Series P-60, No. 114), Washington, D.C.: U.S. Government Printing Office, 1978, pp. 143, 145.

These high-paying jobs in a free and open and equitable society would have contributed two-thirds of the total income received by the population of blacks and other minorities if there had been as many racial minorities as there should have been in these jobs; those who managed to get employment in them were paid on the average one-fifth less than whites who held similar positions. Thus, these four high-paying occupational categories accounted for only one-third of the total income for blacks and other racial-minority households, because of the limitations imposed by racial discrimination.

Unlike the white population, in which two-thirds of the income for the group came from these higher-paying jobs, the black population received two-thirds of its income from the lower status occupations. It is fair to say on the basis of these findings that the black community continues to be supported largely by the wealth of its blue-collar workers.

Despite the increase in education of blacks, the data revealed that only 3 percent of the managers and administrators came from black or other minority household heads in 1976; that there were two-thirds fewer than there should have been; and that, collectively, they earned $9.5 billion less than they would have earned had there not been any discrimination in the number of minorities employed in these occupations and in the salaries thay they received. This occupational category showed the highest discrepancy between what was and should have been; it was followed by professional and technical workers, for whom the discrepancy was down $6.9 billion from what it should have been. The depressed income of the white-collar and skilled workers contributed more significantly to the $17.6 billion income deficit that black and other minorities experienced because of discrimination than did wages received or the overrepresentation in numbers of minorities in blue-collar occupations.

Because $17.6 billion in 1976 would have come to black and other minorities had they not been discriminated against, I conclude that race is significantly associated with these outcomes and continues to influence the income and occupational life-chances of the racial minorities and of the majority in this nation, including the affluent as well as the poorer sectors of their populations, and that the economic effect of racial discrimination for blacks is greater among the affluent than among the poor.

With reference to poor blacks and poor whites who are employed in the low-status occupations of service work, there was little, if any, difference in the education of blacks and of whites who were, for example, barbers, cooks, hairdressers, practical nurses, and waiters (Newman 1978:90). Yet the median family income for black and other minority household heads employed in these and other service occupations in 1976 was one-third less than the median income of whites in these same low-prestige jobs. If race is not an appropriate explanation, why is it that whites of limited education are paid one-third more than blacks who are as qualified as they are? Newman and associates point out that "Blacks had achieved 94 percent of whites' educational position by 1974 and 1975, compared with 79 percent in 1940. But whatever the year, blacks' occupational position did not match their educational position." (Newman 1978:49).

There is social differentiation among blacks as well as among whites in the United States. And the stratification range in terms of median income by occupational groups is similar for both racial populations. Whites who are professionals and who are at the top of the occupational hierarchy receive a median annual income that is approximately twice as much as that received by whites who are poor. And blacks who are professionals receive a median annual income that is about twice as much as that received by blacks who are poor. Because the range of the stratification hierarchy as defined here is similar for both racial populations, why is it that only 1 out of every 10 whites is poor compared to around 3 out of every 10 blacks? The differential rate of poverty between blacks and whites cannot be explained as being a function of the increased social class differentiation of the black population when the white population is differentiated just as much as the blacks and has experienced social class differentiation even longer than the blacks. Despite the differentiation of the white population by social class, its rate of poverty has continued to decrease. Thus, the social class differentiation of a population is no impediment to reducing the size of its underclass, as Wilson has suggested.

The clinical or case-study evidence derived from press reports and the findings from scientific surveys lead to the conclusions that race continues to be significant in the United States; that federal laws such as the Civil Rights Act of 1964 and the Voting Rights Act of 1965 are beginning to have an effect because of recent enforcement efforts of the Justice Department but that they have not come near to eliminating split labor markets or local elections that divide along racial lines; and that the new racial battleground shaping up for the future has to do with political control of local governments in which single-member district elections are advocated by black and by brown populations to wrest control from whites, and at-large elections and city-county consolidation of institutions such as schools and government are advocated by some whites as a means of retaining control. Finally, this analysis has suggested that racial discrimination rather than a limited education is what holds blacks back and contributes to inequality in employment and income.

We come now to the point of determining what this all means in terms of race relations. To recapitulate, a major daily newspaper wishes to retire from our language and common usage the words racist and racism because — it asserts — they are no longer descriptive of race relations in this nation. The white mayor of a big city criticizes a court decision that sanctions a 10 percent reservation of public works programs for minority contractors and attempts to resist a court order that requires the hiring of minorities in a police department that had one of the lowest percentages of minorities in the country. A federal judge states that a finding of discrimination in the hiring of women and minorities for high-level court jobs is more accurate than inaccurate. A major bank in which racial minorities are less than 1 percent of its work force at the managerial level claims that it has not been remiss in hiring and promoting people in black and in brown racial populations. The first black mayor to win an election in a large Alabama city is supported by only 1 out of every 10 white voters.

These facts appear to indicate that most individuals of the majority race have little, if any, feelings of guilt about the unfair ways that racial minorities have been treated in this nation. In this connection guilt is to the social system what pain is to the organic system — a signal that something is amiss, a warning that something is wrong. By acknowledging pain and dealing with that which caused it, corrective action can be taken in time to prevent permanent harm to the organic system. To suppress pain is to deal with the symptom rather than with the cause. Likewise, if we acknowledge and accept guilt as a signal that something is wrong in the social system and take appropriate corrective actions, we may avoid permanent damage of our society. Both the suppression of pain and the repression of guilt can be fatal.

The continuing significance of race is that it is one of the most sensitive and sure indicators of the presence or absence of justice in our society. To repress the guilt of racial discrimination through denial and other means is to permit injustice to fester and erupt from time to time in race riots and other forms of rebellion.

Our society has not learned how to deal with guilt because it has not learned how to listen to minorities who experience the conditions that should stimulate guilt. Those who are best capable of helping a society to expiate its guilt are those who suffer because of injustice — the minorities. However, our society will listen to minorities only when they think and speak like the majority.

Years ago in the *New York Times Magazine,* Arthur Schlesinger, Jr. wrote this: "So let us listen more carefully to our losers. A revolution does not have to succeed to make a point. Victory does not render a [person] infallible nor [one's] ideas invincible. 'Success,' said Nietzsche, 'has always been a great liar' " (Schlesinger 1972:62).

Meditating upon success and failure, Theodore Isaac Rubin, the psychiatrist, said: "We must fight for the right to lose. If we don't accept the right to lose, then we so fear failure that we curtail realistic and attainable desires. ... But despite this obvious reality, our culture stands rigidly against failure and loss, looks upon loss ... as an insult to the human condition" (Rubin 1975:206). For this reason, we defer to those in charge — members of the majority — and will not listen to those who are subdominant, our many minorities. As Schlesinger said, let us listen more carefully to our losers. They, in the end, may be our salvation. The Scriptures assert that the meek shall have the earth as their possession. This is an interesting hypothesis worthy of further study and examination, particularly with reference to the question of race and its dominant and subdominant populations, and the meaning of their presence for the whole nation.

REFERENCES

Boston Globe. 1980. "Police Set Five-Year Goal: 27 New Black Sergeants." (July 10), p. 16.

Boston Globe. 1979. "Birmingham, the End of 'Never.'" (November 2), p. 14.

Brink, Williams, and Louis Harris. 1966. *Black and White.* New York: Simon and Schuster.

Civil Rights Commission, U.S. 1978. *Social Indicators of Equality for Minorities and Women.* Washington: U.S. Government Printing Office.

Dallas Morning News. 1979. "Racist, Schmaist." (September 23).

Fletcher, Joseph. 1966. *Situation Ethics.* Philadelphia: Westminster Press.

Keniston, Kenneth, et al. 1977. *All Our Children.* New York: Harcourt Brace Jovanovich.

Margolis, Richard. 1979. "If We Won, Why Aren't We Smiling." In *The Caste and Class Controversy,* edited by C. V. Willie. Bayside, N.Y.: General Hall.

Newman, Dorothy K. 1979. "Unclass: An Appraisal." In *The Caste and Class Controversy,* edited by C. V. Willie. Bayside, N.Y.: General Hall.

New York Times 1980. July 15: Letter by Dorothy J. Samuels, Executive Director, New York Civil Liberties Union; July 9, "Cincinnati Police to Hire More Blacks and Women," p. A12; June 1, "Courts' Own Data Show Minority Job Exclusion," p.44.

New York Times 1979. November 5, "Dallas Suit on Job Bias Is Viewed as Far Reaching," p. A17; November 1, "Birmingham Victor Elated and Determined,", p. A18; November 1, "Minorities' Influence Will Rise Next Week in Houston's Election," pp. l, B24.

Rawls, John. 1971. *A Theory of Justice.* Cambridge: Harvard University

Press.

Rubin, Theodore Isaac. 1975. *Compassion and Self-Hate*. New York: Ballantine Books.

Schlesinger, Jr., Arthur. 1972. "The Power of Positive Losing." *New York Times Magazine* (June 22).

Sloan, Lee, and Robert M. French. 1977. "Black Rule in the Urban South?" In *Black/Brown/White Relations,* edited by C. V. Willie. New Brunswick, N.J.: Transaction Books.

Tournier, Paul. 1962. *Guilt and Grace*. New York: Harper and Row (first published in 1958).

U.S. Census Bureau. 1978. *Money Income in 1979 in Family and Persons in the United States*. P-60, no. 114. Washington, D.C.: U.S. Government Printing Office (July).

Willie, Charles V. 1980. *Leadership Development for Minorities, An Evaluation of a Rockefeller Foundation Program* (June).

Wilson, William Julius. 1978. *The Declining Significance of Race,* Chicago: University of Chicago Press.

PART II

Case Studies of Black Families: Affluent, Working-Class, and Poor

4 AFFLUENT, WORKING-
CLASS, AND POOR BLACK
FAMILIES: AN OVERVIEW

AFFLUENT BLACKS: The Conformists

The affluent, or middle-class, population among blacks is increasing but it is still relatively small in size — about one out of every three black families. The influence of the members of these families within the black community and upon the society at large is extensive and therefore merits our attention. Affluent or middle-class status for most black families is a result of dual employment of husband and wife. Black men and women have relied heavily on the public sector for employment at livable wages.

The public school has been an employment haven for black working wives. It has provided steady and continuous work and often has been the first professional occupational role in black households. Because of job-connected requirements, black female teachers in middle-class families may be more highly educated than their male spouses. The length of employment of professional working wives is likely to be as long as that of their husbands, with only brief interruptions for child-bearing. The number of children in black middle-class families tends to be small, ranging from one to three, but more often two or less. Thus, the black woman in a public sector job with prescribed yearly increments and retirement benefits, with only a few interruptions in her labor force status, tends to have significant earnings by the time she reaches middle age.

Continuity in employment also is a characteristic of black men in affluent households. Public sector jobs, especially in the postal service, have been a source of support and security over the years. A few black men, however, occupy financially rewarding business and professional positions in industry, education, and as self-employed private practitioners.

The economic foundation for most affluent black families is a product of the cooperative work of the husband and wife. Their way of life is an illustration of a genuine team effort. Few if any family functions, including cooking, cleaning, and shopping, are considered to be the exclusive prerogative of the husband or the wife. Probably the best example of the liberated woman in American society is found in the wife in the black middle-class family. She and her husband have acted as partners out of necessity and thus have carved out an equalitarian pattern of interaction in which neither husband nor wife has ultimate authority. Because of racial discrimination and the income limitations of the kind of jobs available to blacks, he or she alone could not achieve a comfortable style of life. Together they are able to make it, and this they have done. Affluent black families in our study have earned annual incomes — usually the joint income of husband and wife — at or above the national median.

Such income is lavishly spent on a home and on the education of children. Unless restricted by racial discrimination, affluent black families tend to trade in older homes for newer structures as their earnings and savings increase. The real expense in housing, however, is in the up-to-date furnishings and modern appliances. For most affluent black families, their home is their castle, and it is outfitted as such.

Because work is so consuming for the husband and wife, little time is left for socializing. Most families have nearby relatives — usually the reason for migrating to a particular city. They visit relatives occasionally, may hold membership in one or two social organizations, participate regularly in church activities, and spend the remainder of their free time in household unkeep and maintenance chores.

In most affluent black families, one spouse almost always is a college graduate. Often both are college graduates who struggled and made great sacrifices to complete their formal education. Not infrequently, college and graduate school are completed on a part-time basis after adulthood and while the husband or wife, who also may be a parent, is employed full-time. Parents who have experienced these struggles and hardships know that their middle-class status, which usually is not achieved until middle age, is directly correlated with their increased education. New jobs, especially public school teaching, and salary increments can be traced directly to the added schooling. Other public sector jobs use variations in level of education to determine qualifications. Thus, education has been a major contributor to occupational upward mobility for blacks employed by government.

Because education and consequently economic affluence are so closely tied together for middle-income black households, parents tend to encourage their offspring to complete schooling. Particularly do they wish their children to go to college immediately after graduating from high school so that they will not have to struggle as long as did their parents, whom middle-class status eluded during young-adult years. An ambition of most parents is to give to their children opportunities that they themselves did not have.

As a starter, almost all children in affluent households are given music lessons. Daughters, in particular, are expected to learn to play a musical instrument, usually the piano. In addition to developing musical and recreational skills, most children in affluent black families are expected to work around the house for an allowance. Most affluent blacks try to inculcate in their children positive attitudes toward work and thrift.

Active involvement in community affairs that takes on the characteristics of a social movement is not the way of life for most middle-class, middle-aged blacks. Black adolescents may be deeply involved in various movements but seldom are their parents. It is difficult to determine whether the low rate of black-adult community participation is due to insufficient energy and time because of the extra demands of joint employment of husband and wife, a belief that their own personal progress is a contribution to community and racial group progress, a desire to disassociate themselves from the struggles of others, or a feeling that their participation and involvement is unwelcomed.

Middle-class black families in the United States manifest probably better than any other population group the Puritan orientation toward work, success, and self-reliance so characteristic of the basic values of this nation. For them, work is a consuming experience. Little time is left for recreation and other kinds of social activities except perhaps regular involvement in church affairs. Based on his analysis of the correlation between religion and economics, Max Weber authored a major work called *The Protestant Ethic and the Spirit of Capitalism* (Weber 1948). The way of life of affluent black Americans is a scenario patterned after the Weberian theory, except that most blacks have little capital other than the house that they own, which, of course, is their primary symbol of success.

In summary, affluent or middle-class black families identify with the basic goals in American society. Family members are achievement-oriented, upwardly mobile, and equalitarian. They immerse themselves in work and have little time for leisure. Personal property, especially residential property, is a major symbol of success. These family members appropriately may be called affluent conformists.

WORKING-CLASS BLACKS: The Innovators

Family life in the black working class is a struggle for survival that requires the cooperative efforts of all — husband, wife, and children. Income for black working-class families in this study ranges from just above the official poverty line to just below the national median. This is hardly enough for luxury living when the family size is considered. Black working-class families tend to be larger than affluent households, consisting of five or more children.

There is some indication that the size of the family is a source of pride for the parents, especially the father, and maybe the mother too. The bearing and rearing of children is considered to be an important citizenship responsibility, so much so that black working-class parents make great personal sacrifices for their families. They tend to look upon children as their unique contribution to society, a creative contribution they are unable to make through their work roles, which at best are semiskilled. The size of the black working-class family also may be related to age at marriage of the parents — usually before 21 years and often during the late teens for the wife and mother. Husbands tend to assume parenthood responsibilities early too; they tend to be only one or two years older than their spouses.

Cohesion in the black working-class family results not so much from understanding and tenderness shown by one for the other as from the joint and heroic effort to stave off adversity. Without the income of either parent or the contributions of off-spring from part-time employment, the family would topple back into poverty.

Parents in black working-class families are literate but have limited education. Most have completed elementary school but may be high school dropouts. Seldom have any gone beyond high school. This is the educational level these parents wish their children to achieve, although some families hope that one or two of the smarter children in their brood will go on to college. The jobs that they wish for their children also are those that require only a high school or junior college education, such as work as a secretary, nurse, or skilled manual worker.

Racial discrimination, on the one hand, and insufficient education on the other have teamed up to delimit the employment opportunities for black working-class households, whose mobility from rural to urban areas and from South to North usually has been in search for a better life. Families tend to be attracted to a particular community because of the presence of relatives, who sometimes provide temporary housing and other relocation assistance.

In general, the moves open up new opportunities and modest advancements such as, for example, from gas station attendant to truck driver. The northern migration has resulted in some disappointments, too; a barber, for example, may be unable to pass the licensure examination to practice his trade and, therefore, becomes a janitor. On balance, new employment opportunities have resulted from the move from South to North, particularly for wives, who have found work in institutional settings such as hospitals more profitable than private household work. Nursing aide, cook, and other semiskilled jobs or service work are outlets for women in the black working class and have enabled these women to supplement the family income.

One sacrifice that the members of black working-class families have made so as to pull out of and stay beyond the clutches of poverty is to give up on doing things together as a family. Long working hours and sometimes two jobs leave little time for the father to interact with family members. In some households the husband may work during the daytime, and the wife, during the evening hours. In other families, children work up to twenty hours a week after school and on weekends. Such work schedules mean that the family as a unit is not able to share any meals together, except possibly on a Sunday.

Despite the hardships, there is a constancy among the members of black working-class families that tends to pull them through. They tend to be long-term residents of their neighborhoods and stable workers with a long work history with one employer. Though their earnings are modest, the family's continuity in area of residence and in other experiences has had a stabilizing influence and has enabled members to accumulate the makings of a tolerable existence without the losses that come from frequent stops and starts.

Another unifying experience is the home that some black working-class families own. Rather than renting, many are paying out mortgages. Home ownership for some is a major family goal. The owned home may be located in an isolated rural or unsightly urban area, and may be in a poor state of repair exteriorly, but it is neat and clean on the inside. Home ownership for black working-class families is not so much a symbol of success as an indicator of respectability.

Black working-class parents boast of the fact that their children are good and have not been in trouble with the police. They also have a strong sense of morality that emphasizes clean living. The home that they own is part of their symbol of stability. The owned home is one blessing that can be counted. It is a haven from the harsh and sometimes unfriendly world.

There is little time for participation in community activities by adults in black working-class families. Most spare time is devoted to associating with household members or with nearby relatives. Religion is important; but participation in church affairs is limited to regular or occasional attendance at Sunday worship services. The mother in such families tries to maintain tenuous contacts with at least one community institution, such as the school. She even may be a member of the school-community council or another similar social service, but she is not deeply involved in work as a volunteer.

Black working-class parents do well by their children if no special problems are presented. Their comprehension of psychological maladaptions is limited. These problems, when they appear, are dealt with by a series of intended remedial actions that seem to be of little assistance in solving the real problem and that usually result in frustration both for the parent and the offspring, or between spouses. Black working-class families have learned to endure; and so they bear with the afflictions of their members — those that they do not understand as well as those with obvious sources of causation.

Cooperation for survival is so basic in black working-class families that relationships between the husband and the wife take on an equalitarian character. Each knows that his or her destiny is dependent upon the actions of the other. Within the family, however, husbands and wives tend to have assigned roles, although in time of crisis these roles can change. The husband tends to make decisions about financial expenditures. He also has responsibility for maintenance of the housing structure. The father is the chief advisor for the boys. The mother tends to be responsible for the cooking and cleaning, although she may delegate these chores to the children. She is the chief advisor for the girls. She also maintains a liaison relationship with the school and may be the adult link between the family and the church if the father is not inclined to participate.

Many working-class black families are households moving out of poverty into "respectability"; they are households that emphasize mobility, goal, and purpose; they are committed to making a contribution to society by raising and maintaining a family of good citizens. This, of course, involves a struggle. But the struggle may be a function of the ending of good times rather than the overcoming of adversity. A black working-class family may be a lower-income household on its way up or a middle-class household on its way down. In black families with limited capital there is little margin for error. A middle-class black family beset with illness, for example, can slip into the working-class status because of reduction in income and the attendant requirement for change in style of living. How often this occurs, we do not know. It does occur often enough to keep the working class from becoming a homogeneous lot. For this and other reasons, one should not expect to find a common philosophical orientation within the working-class.

In summary, the black working-class family also is an example of a household that has internalized the basic American values. Not being able to make a creative contribution through their work roles, black working-class parents consider the rearing of respectable and well-behaved children as their major contribution to the community. They therefore emphasize the fact that they are stable, that they can be counted on, and that none in their household has been in trouble with public authorities.

Black working-class families with limited education and occupational opportunities are ingenious in their methods of coping, surviving, and overcoming adversity. From multiple employment of the household head to dual employment of husband and wife that requires tandem parenting, they find a way. The means used to cope are tailor-made for each household and are most innovative. The black working class is a conglomerate group consisting of poor families on their way up and middle-class families on their way down. They probably are the best manifestation of self-reliance in American society. They are sustained by few institutional supports beyond the kinship system. By hook or crook they make it when others say, "it can't be done." *The ones who make it when it seems impossible. Innovators*

POOR BLACKS: The Rebels

The most important fact about poor black families is their

low-income status. They therefore are forced to make a number of necessary, clever, and sometimes foolish arrangements to exist. These arrangements represent their rebellion against common goals and conventional ways of doing things in society. These range from extended households consisting of several generations under one roof to taking in boarders or foster children for pay. "Boyfriend-girlfriend" relationships between adults often assume parental functions when children are involved, while the participants maintain their autonomy unfettered by marital bonds. Because every penny counts, poor households often do whatever they must do to bring the money in. Conventional practices of morality may be set aside for expedient arrangements that offer the hope of a livable existence. The struggle among poor families is a struggle for existence. All else is secondary. Family income is near or less than the official federal poverty line. Some families cannot survive without public welfare.

The struggle is severe and there is no margin for error. Poor black families learn to live with contingency. They hope for little and expect less. Parents love their children but seldom understand them. Men and women become sexually involved but are afraid to entrust their futures to each other. There is much disappointment. The parents in broken families sometimes have broken spirits — too broken to risk serious involvement with another mate and possible another disappointment. For this reason black lower-class parents often appear to be uncommitted to anyone or to anything when in actuality they are afraid to trust.

Movement is constant, as if they were trying to get away from something, as if they would be caught by someone if they settled down. Jobs, houses, and communities are changed, and so are spouses and boyfriends or girlfriends. Unemployment is a constant specter. The womenfolk in the households usually find employment as maids and private household workers or in other service occupations that require few skills. The males are unskilled factory workers or maintenance men between periods of no work at all.

Marriage may occur at an early age, as early as sixteen

years for some girls. The first child may be born before the first marriage, or pregnancy may be the reason for marriage. Other children tend to come in rapid succession. Some families have as many as eight or more children, while others are smaller. The size of the family often is a function of the number of years of marriage. First marriages may dissolve after three or four years. Other marriages or arrangements may follow. When the burdens of more children, illness, and unemployment strike at the same time, they often are overwhelming. Drinking, gambling, and other escape behavior may increase. A fragile love and capacity for endurance are shattered and the man in the house moves out or the woman elopes, no longer able to take it. One more failure is experienced.

The parents in poor black families are grade school or high school dropouts. Neither spouse has much more education than the other. Thus, parents in lower-class families sometimes hold themselves up to their children as failures, as negative images of what not to do. There is only limited ability to give guidance concerning what ought to be done. Children are advised not to marry early, not to drop out of school, and not to do this and not to do that. There is admonition but little concrete effort at prevention.

Scapegoating is a common way of explaining deviant behavior in children. Juvenile delinquency may be attributed to a disreputable parent. The mother on location seldom knows what to do. Although little love may exist between parents, there is fierce loyalty between mothers and offspring, and grandmothers, too. The children come first. Mothers will extend every effort to take care of their sons and daughters even into adulthood. Grandparents are excellent babysitters. They are expected to teach their grandchildren good manners and other fundamentals.

Also, a strong custom exists of brothers and sisters helping each other. The problem is that siblings often are struggling too. About the most one can do for the other is share already overcrowded living quarters when a new member comes to town or when a two-parent family breaks down. The move from one city to another often is for the purpose of being near kin. There is strong loyalty among siblings, and a standing obligation to help.

Little participation in any community association is seen. Religion is important for some poor families, but for others, it is no more than a delusion. Those who attend church regularly are engulfed with religion. They affirm its saving grace and reward system after death. Some shy away from the church as one more disappointing promise that has copped out on the poor without helping. Poor blacks are seldom lukewarm about religion. They are either all for it or all against it, although the latter are reluctant to deny their children religious experience, just in case there is more to it than was realized.

It is hard for a poor black family to overcome poverty; so much is lined up against it. If illness or unemployment do not drain away resources, there is a high probability that old age will.

In summary, poor black families are rebellious. They reject the society that has rejected them. Their rejection is often passive but sometimes active to the point of riotous behavior. Failure and disappointment recur regularly as if they were a refrain. Because the black poor have been given so little, they have not learned how to receive — which is to say, they have not learned how to trust. Thus, they appear to be uncommitted to anyone or anything. However, mothers are loyal to their offspring, and brothers and sisters have a standing obligation to help each other. Men sometimes act as fathers even when they are afraid to risk the commitment of marriage. Most poor families hope for a better day. But when the hope of the black poor is taken away, violent rebellion is their method of resisting; it is a costly way of changing things, including the institutions of a repressive society.

REFERENCE

Weber, Max. 1948. *The Protestant Ethic and the Spirit of Capitalism.* London: Allen and Unwin.

5 AFFLUENT CONFORMISTS

The family patterns of six affluent black households are presented in this chapter. All are two-parent families in which both husband and wife work. The husband and the wife have both finished college in all six families. In two of the six, at least one spouse has earned a doctoral degree; all told, four of the six have one or more spouses who have received graduate education. In the Newsom family, the husband is a physician and the wife, a physical therapist; the father in the Bellows household is a public administrator in city government and the mother, a teacher in a publicly supported college. The Miller children have an engineer in industry and a public school teacher as parents; and the Hines household includes a letter carrier and a public school teacher. Mr. and Mrs. Phillips also share the post office and the schoolroom, although Mr. Phillips is a postal clerk, not a letter carrier. Both husband and wife are public school teachers in the Emerson family. These reports of family patterns have been prepared by undergraduate and graduate students, with only minor editing. They are fresh in perspective, devoid of cant, and presented with honesty and sympathy.

HEALTHY AND WEALTHY, BUT NOT HAPPY
Dennis Ashby

It was the first time that I had met this family, and the atmosphere surrounding the session was quite pleasant. I left the interview pleased with what had been accomplished. The interview took place in St. Louis, in the home of Dr. and Mrs. Harry Newsom. The father and stepmother are parents of Tami — the middle child in the family who arranged for the interview. The mood of the parents was very receptive and cordial.

We spoke for about an hour and a half about the various problems faced by this family. The head of the household is Dr. Harry Newsom, a dentist. He is self-employed and his office is in a business district of St. Louis. His wife, Sylvia, also works, as a physical therapist in a private hospital in St. Louis. These two jobs contribute to a family income that is quite satisfactory.

Sylvia Newsom is Dr. Newsom's second wife. The children in the family were from the first marriage of Dr. Newsom. It ended in divorce. Richard is the oldest of the Newsom three, then Tami and finally Ruth. Ruth lives with her grandmother. She has lived with her grandmother since the divorce several years ago. Richard was living in an apartment in St. Louis but recently moved back home for financial reasons. Tami is the other daughter, who now resides in Boston, Massachusetts. She is presently a senior at Boston University.

All three offspring have been provided with good educations. Dr. Newsom has been described as being extremely hard with his children concerning their school progress. Grades were very important throughout high school. Richard has completed three years of college, but has now taken a leave of absence. He left school to work for a newspaper and live on his own. Eventually he plans to return to school and finish college. He, too, wishes to go into dentistry, which requires college and graduate school. Richard is excellent in sciences and mathematics. He is majoring in chemistry. His decision to go into dentistry is his

59

own. Dr. Newsom did not try to direct any of his children toward any particular profession.

Tami, as I mentioned, is in her fourth year at Boston University. She transferred there after a year at Western Reserve University. When she first enrolled in Western Reserve her grades fell. She attributed this to being away from home without her father's presence to force her to study. She attended a junior college to pull her grades back up, and was then accepted at Boston University for her sophomore year. She will graduate in June. Tami states that she has no immediate plans for the future, but will probably work during the summer, and then continue her education at Boston University in a graduate counseling program. Afte that, nothing is definite.

The youngest of the three, Ruth, finished high school last year. She then enrolled in a junior college for only one semester. The second semester there was a teacher's strike. During this period she left school. She has applied to other schools and hopes to continue her education in September wherever she is accepted. Presently, her only plans are to return to school as soon as possible and finish at least her initial four years.

Dr. Newsom attended a junior college before going on to complete his college and graduate work at the University of Missouri. Sylvia Newsom also did graduate work. She attended Washington University and completed three years of graduate school. Both husband and wife are good examples that education does pay off, and apparently this feeling is being transferred to their children.

This present marriage has been in progress for about twelve years. Sylvia Newsom, as stated earlier, is the stepmother of all three Newsom children. The first marriage of Dr. Newsom ended in divorce when Tami, the middle child, was a preschooler. After the divorce, all three children moved in with their grandmother. Richard and Tami rejoined their father after he married Sylvia and established a new household. The first Mrs. Newsom is now deceased.

The relations within the family are strained due to the divorce, the living arrangements after the divorce, the creation of a new household, and the death of the natural mother of the children. As an indication of estrangement, most members of the family eat dinner alone. There is no specific hour for dining when everyone gathers, except perhaps for breakfast. Tami's father has never taken time from his work to visit her at her college. He has promised to visit but has not appeared. She is uncertain whether he will be on hand for her graduation. He sends money to his children when they ask for it. The children feel that material wealth is shared with them by their father rather than love and kindness.

The husband and wife in the Newsom family lead relatively quiet lives, as is indicated by their weekend and weekly schedules. On a normal Sunday, Dr. Newsom describes his schedule as eating three meals a day, reading books and newspapers, and watching television. Mrs. Newsom does the cooking for the household and also does housework, since she works away from home during the week. On weekends, Richard often visits his friends after lunch and Tami visits her friends also or stays home and reads or watches television.

On an ordinary weekday, Dr. Newsom has breakfast early and is off to his office. Following work and dinner that evening, he usually watches television for a while. Mrs. Newsom follows a similar schedule — an early breakfast an then off to work. At night, she cooks dinner and relaxes afterward by enjoying television also. Richard either attends classes or goes to work. When Tami is at home during vacation time, she does very little and relaxes.

Dr. Newsom is originally from Texas and his wife, Sylvia, is from Idaho. Both moved to St. Louis many years ago. Since living in St. Louis, they have done quite well financially. They have a family income well over the national median and live quite comfortably. They live in a racially mixed neighborhood in a rather large house that has ten rooms altogether, including four bedrooms, a kitchen, a living room, a dining room, plus two bathrooms and a library. It is a single-family home that the Newsom household owns. All of today's luxuries are to be found in and around the house.

Dr. Newsom and his family know between ten and twenty people in his neighborhood, and he says he likes the neighborhood because of the friendly people. However, he is think-ing of moving elsewhere in the St. Louis metropolitan area because of the "large amount of noise" in the current neigh-borhood that is disturbing, and also because of their recent ex-perience of thefts and break-ins. The present neighborhood he classifies as "an average area."

Regarding family members' roles in this household, the mother chooses the foods for the family and cooks the meals, decorates the home, and makes decisions about home fur-nishings. The father decides what house and car the family would buy. Difficulties with children at school were always left to Dr. Newsom. He always spoke to his children's teachers con-cerning their progress in class. He states that he has a little in-fluence as to what political candidates he and his wife vote for. Otherwise, both parents shared in raising their offspring. When the children are sick, both mother and father take care of them. The teaching of manners is a responsibility assumed by both parents. And when there was work to do, both parents assigned chores to the children.

Many aspects of the children's lives were left entirely up to them. They did their own homework, although their father often made them do it but did not help them with it. The father paid for the education of his children but they chose their own schools. They spent their allowance money as they wished. They chose their own clothes, and what to wear on a specific day. They also were left to decide on any particular religion they wished to try, if any at all.

Although Dr. Newsom's preference is Protestant and Mrs. Newsom's is Catholic, neither go to church on a regular basis. They have not attempted to influence their children regarding religious preferences.

Dr. and Mrs. Newsom are not very much into any types of community organizations. As I mentioned, they lead a rather quiet life; after working hard all day, they do little else but relax. Dr. Newsom is, however, a member of the National Dental Association, which is the black counterpart of the American Dental Association. Otherwise, the Newsoms are not connected with any church or secret societies or civil rights groups or the like.

This family has enough money to afford luxuries and can afford a private family home. This does not necessarily lead to happiness for all the family members, however. In the United States material wealth is all important. It is sad that the gaining of material wealth may leave little time for understanding one's own children. This seems to be a problem in the Newsom household. As the children grow up in this affluent black family, it seems that the family split is widening instead of coming closer together.

It is often assumed, too, that only poor families get divorced or separated. A great majority of black families are thought to be welfare recipients. And, black people are normally associated with run-down communities called ghettoes. Yet, here we find quit an exception. Here is a family in which the mother and father have several years of graduate school work between them, which shows better than average education. Both have fine jobs that are considered highly respectable. And money is not lacking. Yet harmony and togetherness are lacking. This family failed at living together. This may be the result of the first divorce, which occurred when the children were young and unable to cope with the major change brought about by a divorce. Little was done to remedy this situation and what began then exists today. When the parents divorced, it seemed that they thought only of themselves and not of their children's welfare.

It is quite strange that the goals Americans strive for most, education and money, do not in themselves provide happiness. This family is a prime example. On the outside one sees a large comfortable home. A father with the title of doctor. A mother who is a physical therapist. All of these point to a sufficient income.

Money can buy homes and cars and television sets, but it can never buy a close relationship within a family. It is too bad that people with a great deal of education can not see and correct their own faults. When I hear white America talking about "get yourself an education and you'll be better off," I often wonder if you really are better off. I know many poor black families who are at least happy despite their lack of education and material wealth. I would much rather know that someone cared about me and to live in a close home than to have all the money in the world. It is really a matter of what means the most to a particular person. From this interview I gained a lot of insight into the minds of people. It was well worth the experience to learn how other black families live.

GRACEFUL LIVING IN GREEN ACRES
Levi Moore

My friend, who was driving me to my point of destination, had high praise for the Green Acres suburban area. He spoke of his own hopes of someday being able to get away from it all. We took the freeway to the Green Acres exit and entered a very modern and beautiful park-terrace shopping area. Spacious with trees and flowers planted in every available spot. We continued through the shopping area, turned off the main road and continued for about two miles along a sparsely settled road until we reached Silver Village. The houses were set back from the road and all of the lawns were immaculate. Children in casually well-groomed, expensive clothing rode bikes or strolled along the streets.

We continued deeper into the division and located the house. A two-story ranch style with a long drive leading to a two-car garage connected to the house by a covered walkway. Parking space was provided to the right of the garage with a wide walkway leading to the front door. The house had the contour of the gently sloping hill on which it was built. Behind the house and extended along the rear of several was a very large lake. I rang the bell and a friendly voice from an intercom above the door asked what it could do for me. I explained that I was the man from Harvard and the voice said it would be with me in a minute. I said good-by to my driver friend and went back to the door. Mr. Bellows opened the door welcoming me to come in and I stepped in a large foyer with steps to my left leading to the second floor. Mr. Bellows, a small man, was very cordial, asking about my trip and my work at school. He seemed really glad to be of help. He said that he had been working on his boat and would need to put up a few things and asked if I'd like to go with him. We walked down a long corridor toward the rear of the house through a huge den and outside. We walked along a covered walkway through a drydock a little distance from the

65

lake to where the boat was moored. The boat slept four people, had its own galley, and was air-jet powered. Mr. Bellows said he had been interested in boats since he was a kid. He often took the boat either for the fishing or just to get away, sometimes with the family. We went back to the house and continued our conversation in the den. The wife and two of the children were away. The housekeeper baby-sitter brought coffee and danish rolls to the den at Mr. Bellows' request.

Mr. Bellows is at the beginning of middle age. He was born in Philadelphia and had lived in the vicinity all of his life. Mrs. Elsie Bellows, six years younger than her husband, was born in South Carolina and had come to Philadelphia to study when they met and subsequently became engaged. They were married in South Carolina. They have three children, a son, Spencer Bellows, Jr., 8 years of age; a daughter, Cynthia, 5 year of age; and another son, Michael, only 1 year old. Mr. Bellows had a Doctor of Education degree and Mrs. Bellows had a master's degree in music. The oldest son, Spencer Jr., was in public elementary school, having spent three years in private school. Cynthia, not yet of school age, was in the same private school kindergarten that Spencer Jr. had attended. Mr. and Mrs. Bellows had no previous marriages and had been married ten years.

Mr. Bellows was responsible for much of the building and contract work for the city of Philadelphia. His work had to do with compliance of contractors, their ability to do certain jobs, special work with minority contractors, needs assessments for certain new construction. He said that his job made it possible to help a lot of minority contractors get work they would not normally have heard of. Mrs. Bellows worked at a local public college. He didn't know exactly what she did but she later told me that she helped the colleges work on improving the music curricula especially for the brighter students. They were good at producing high school music teachers she said, but the bright students really had to go on to private school. She had studied at a private school.

Mr. Bellows was Protestant and never attended church except on festive or celebratory occasions that involved the children. Mrs. Bellows was a Catholic and attended services regularly. The children were also Catholic and attended services with the mother. Mrs. Bellows was to tell me later that her family had practically built the church in the South Carolina city where she grew up.

Mr. Bellows described the family as close but said he did not get out with the children as much as the mother. Of children and the police, he said that the security patrol, paid by the community, kept down the pranks, mostly speeding, to a minimum. The kids did well in school especially as far as grades and deportment were concerned, but he'd just have to spend more time with Spencer Jr. to toughen him up a little. The mother did what little disciplining that needed to be done, but he thought the children took advantage sometimes. There was no regular time for eating supper and only the mother and children ate breakfast and dinner together regularly. The children were transported to school and other activities by private car. The children normally studied their homework after dinner in the family room. This helps to develop good habits, Mrs. Bellows said. She liked to visit the school whenever she could, and she had had the principal to dinner. The children, she said, would all be professional workers. She would really like one to be a doctor and one to be a lawyer.

Mr. Bellows talked freely about their family income, which he estimated at more than twice the national median. His father, he said, had given him a good start in real estate. The tax shelter helpted out also, if the houses don't pay, deduct, he said. Both were completely satisfied with the neighborhood, they enjoyed the sense of neighborliness of all the people living there. They could be depended on to watch your property, check your mail, and see that your lawn was kept when you were away. They also exchanged tools, recipes, and sometime even kept each other's children.

They wanted to stay in the neighborhood because it seemed to be child oriented and the public schools were very good and they were close to recreation for the entire family. They are member of a local club that is quite expensive but that provides good leisure activities, including a private golf course.

They classify the neighborhood as an upper class, white one because of the few nonwhites living there. Mrs. Bellows does not think that children in the neighborhood are necessarily well behaved, and thinks the whites believe in too much cheap psychology. She felt that both the private and public police did a good job.

The single-family home and grounds on which it was located was quite valuable. The house had a kitchen, three bedrooms with baths, nursery, living room, dining room, breakfast room, family room, recreation room, den, and a hobby room for Mrs. Bellows, music room, and basement. There were several color televisions in the house, several with wall-size projectors. There was an intercom system throughout the house adapted to a stereo-phono-tape set. They subscribed to several magazines, several daily papers, as well as *Better Homes, Changing Times, Jet,* and *Ebony.* They had several telephones with a separate line for the children. The best features of the neighborhood is that it is safe, convenient, and with plenty of space. They would both like to have more blacks in the neighborhood, but said the racial ratio is typical.

Mrs. Bellows knew from five to ten people but Mr. Bellows knew from twenty to thirty. Both would turn to their respective families if they needed help. The wife's family were land owners and bankers. The husband's father was in the retail liquor business and real estate.

They both felt that the community provided equal opportunity, excellent education, cultural opportunities. They felt that recreation and community organizations could be improved but were not too satisfied with the predominantly white government officials.

They both contributed generously to community chest, church, and many other charitable purposes. They both served on boards and had leadership responsibility for civic improvement. They were both declared Democrats and were very active in the past and the present national political campaigns. They were both very vocal on the needs and shortcomings of government and governmental institutions. They were regular voters and voted two to five times in the last four years. They both wrote, spoke, and visited congressmen several times, and were very concerned over the qualifications needed for public office.

Mrs. Bellows' leisure time activity was chiefly around the family, which she most liked to do along with weekly bridge with her club on a regular basis. Mr. Bellows liked to hunt deer and fish in Canada, which he did annually. He also liked camping and had a vacation lodge accessible by boat where he went fairly often with two other friends. Both had traveled extensively in foreign countries.

Mrs. Bellows, a very beautiful woman, had returned home in the early afternoon with the two servants, who commuted to the house daily. They prepared the meals and kept the house. Mrs. Bellows supervised the shopping, and principally ran the home. The decor was obviously Old South.

The conversation automatically turned to her on her arrival. Mr. Bellows took the kids out on the grounds to the playground elaborately equipped with a miniature basketball court, swings, slides, etc.

I remained for a very elaborate dinner which we all ate together, had wine and cigarettes in the den, and waited for my friend to pick me up.

THE LONELY SELF-INTEGRATORS
Michael Rettig

The Millers live in a nicely furnished house about ten blocks east of the University. When I came to visit, Mrs. Miller had just returned from the beauty salon and she and her nine-year-old daughter Sandy were listening to records on a beautiful component stereo (Harmon and Kardon, Daul and Fisher). We immediately got to talking about jazz and Mrs. Miller told me how Sandy had once stunned her uncle by asking him if he "dug Dave Brubeck."

Mr. and Mrs. Miller both hail from a suburb of Pittsburgh, Pennsylvania. They both grew up in a racially mixed neighborhood and attended mixed schools. She said, presumably with no degradation intended, that they grew up with a bunch of "honkies" who were their friends, enemies, and classmates. Although her family wasn't well to do, Mrs. Miller told me that they never went hungry. The church played a large part in their growth and development with both Mr. and Mrs. Miller attending Baptist services, as, Mrs. Miller chucklingly put it, "God-fearing people." After he left the home of his parents, Mr. Miller stopped going to church. Graduating from high school, Mrs. Miller attended a small college with a predominantly white student body in Pennsylvania. She was one of the three blacks in a freshman class of 300 students. The majority of her friends were white and during these years she had little social contact with blacks at school. Mr. Miller also attended college and graduated with a degree in electrical engineering. Continuing her studies after graduation, Mrs. Miller took the necessary courses for certification in elementary education. She also joined an honorary black sorority in Pittsburgh. A year after her graduation from college, Mr. and Mrs. Miller were married.

The Millers are an affluent family. Having taught school for ten years, Mrs. Miller earns a good salary from the Rochester school district, while Mr. Miller works as an electrical engineer. Their combined income is about twice the national median. When she saw the highest category of earnings on the interview schedule, Mrs. Miller remarked, "I almost earn that myself." Their life as a family has been characterized by a great deal of movement due to Mr. Miller's job. In fact, at the end of this school year they are moving back to Pittsburgh, this time for a different reason (to be discussed later). Mrs. Miller usually enjoys teaching, but in the interview she stated frustratingly that, "inner city kids are a different breed of kid. They have no motivation and I don't know how to get them going." She is the only black teacher in the school and again all her friends are white (at school).

Although he enjoys his job, Mr. Miller has had to work a great deal lately. He must be on the job at 8:00 a.m. and often he doesn't return until after 8:00 p.m. (In fact, the night I interviewed the family Mr. Miller had not yet returned when I left at 9:30.) Both Mr. and Mrs. Miller seemed very diligent at their work and rarely miss work because of sickness. Their hard work has paid off, at least materially. Besides the new stereo, I observed two cars, a piano for Sandy, and a beautifully furnished house.

The Millers are a close family. This was manifest (to me) in Sandy's hanging all over her mother during parts of the interview. Their closeness could be a function of both the loving state of the family and the great amount of moving the family has done in the last few years. When you don't live in an area for a long time it is difficult to form long-lasting relationships outside of the family. This makes for increased contact among the members of the family.[1] Unable to eat breakfast and lunch together because of different schedules, the Millers try to eat dinner together even though Mr. Miller sometimes works late. (I discovered when I was leaving that Mrs. Miller and Sandy had not yet eaten).

After Sandy and Mrs. Miller return from their respective

---

[1]This could be an erroneous generalization, but it seems true in the Miller family because neither the parents nor Sandy have any strong outside relationships.

schools, Mrs. Miller begins cooking and then spends a lot of the time before dinner talking to Sandy about her school day or just giving general motherly attention. On the weekends much of the free time is spent on individual pursuits. Sandy reads, does homework, watches television, or practices the piano. Mrs. Miller might read, watch TV, or do her lesson plans, while Mr. Miller is often found listening to records and reading in the living room. Mrs. Miller told me that often after a hard day's work, she would find her husband asleep in his chair with a book on his chest.

Although Mrs. Miller makes many everyday decisions, husband and wife join together to make the major family decisions, such as: where to live, what car to buy, and the upbringing of their daughter. It should be mentioned that Mrs. Miller is the one who made the decision to have only one child.

The Millers chose to bring Sandy up in a disciplined manner. Thus she must do her homework, practice piano (not excessively), and always obey. Mrs. Miller feels that she is leading her daughter to be an independent person because she has "no time to pamper her." This method of child-rearing could be the cause of Sandy's advanced achievement in school (not to mention the fact that her mother is a teacher). Mrs. Miller seemed very proud of her daughter's performance in the classroom as she told me, that although in the third grade, she was reading on fifth-grade level. Both mother and daughter complained that the kids fooled around too much. Sandy told me that, "One day the teacher gave us a sheet to do and I started right away. Then the girl behind me yelled out, 'Sandy's up to 24 already!' The teacher gave me a new sheet and told me to start over again." Mrs. Miller has met with the teacher at both PTA meetings and the parent-teacher home conference. The above reprimand was typical of what Sandy thought of her teacher and classmates. Another reason for Sandy's low opinion of teacher and classmates could be the contrast between the public school she is attending now and the private schools she has attended in the past. The move from private to public schools was made because Mr. Miller didn't want his daughter to live a sheltered life. As far as her daughter's future was concerned, Mrs. Miller put the emphasis on what Sandy wanted, as long as it was in the professional vein. Having once visited a female doctor's office, Sandy was all excited about the prospect of being a doctor, even though she knew it entailed eight years of schooling after she was finished with high school.

Because the Millers have just been living in the neighborhood a few months, as I said before, they have not had a chance to form any very close relationships outside of the family. When Mrs. Miller was asked how many people she knew in the area she could only cite ten. There was not much said about Sandy's social life, but playing with friends was not mentioned. In case the family ever needed outside help, Mrs. Miller said she would probably first call her minister. Because, she said, "he is a sympathetic and helpful man." Both mother and daughter attend church regularly while Mr. Miller only goes on special holidays, such as, Christmas and Easter. Although Mrs. Miller and Sandy do go to church they have been too involved in the settling process to be able to participate in church-organized community activities. Mrs. Miller does have one other friend, a woman she met registering for a graduate course at the University. "She is the only black person who has been in the house since we've moved in," Mrs. Miller told me.

The neighborhood the Millers live in is satisfactory in every way except for the fact that Mrs. Miller wishes there were more black people in the area. She likes the neighborhood because, as she said, "The people are home owners, they take pride in their house and yard." Also she commented that it was a "quiet neighborhood with no buggy kids and no police problems." No member of the family has become active in community affairs mainly because of the short period of their residence.

The Millers are returning to a suburb of Pittsburgh. This move is being made for a combination of reasons headed by their dislike of Rochester. They have met few friendly people in this city. She couldn't describe her bad feelings, but perhaps it is analogous to a mild case of a midwesterner moving to the east. Another motivation for the move is Mrs. Miller's dislike of teaching inner-city children, and the fact, that except for in church and for the small children in school, "the family is not exposed to enough black people in the course of a day." They seem eager to leave the area.

After finishing the interview schedules, I felt as though we had built up a good enough rapport to talk about her views on present-day race relations. We talked freely about times when racist attitudes might have affected her family. It turned out that she never really had been exposed to such views. Having grown up in a mixed and liberal suburb, Mrs. Miller was never overtly confronted with racial hostility. Even at a predominantly white college there was little tension. She did mention that when Mr. Miller was looking for a house to rent in Rochester, he had encountered some jacked up prices. Mrs. Miller admitted being unable to identify with the poorer blacks in this country who are struggling for survival within the racist system. She and her family, in the upper echelon of society, have never been hungry and have always had the money to pay their own way.

When talking about radical black movements, Mrs. Miller came out against any type of extreme action. She felt that extremists' militant action would not "change the minds of the whites." Resigned to a slow evolutionary process, Mrs. Miller saw the solution to American's race problems in the actions of "good whites, like the Kennedy brothers, and blacks such as Martin Luther King, Jr."

Her students, Mrs. Miller told me, were a part of the "welfare generation." She based this thought on her experience with free lunch tickets granted by the Welfare Department. It turned out that 15 of the 18 children in her class who stayed for lunch received free lunch tickets. Mrs. Miller felt that the parents of inner-city children didn't care about their children and didn't provide an enviornment at home conducive to learning in school. Continuing about her students, Mrs. Miller said that many of the white teachers were afraid of repercussions from severe disciplining of black students on race charges, but that she could treat them as they deserved without that fear.

THE POSTMAN AND THE PUBLIC SCHOOL TEACHER
Beryl M. Dakers

Mr. and Mrs. Hines have been married twenty-four years. Both parents are employed full-time. Mr. Hines is a letter carrier for the U.S. Post Office and Mrs. Hines is a high school science teacher, employed by the City School System. The family's income is slightly above the national median. To supplement his stable income, Mr. Hines often seeks extra employment as a yard man. The children are also employed in various part-time jobs to cover their minor personal expenses.

Mr. Hines was born in Atlanta, Georgia. Orphaned at age eight, he was raised by an uncle and aunt who had twelve children of their own and little extra money or love to spare on an additional child. He vividly recalls the trials of this early childhood, particularly the pangs of poverty and hunger. At age seventeen, Mr. Hines came to Raleigh, North Carolina to work his way through college. He did this by securing a number of indiscriminate and often low-paying jobs. Majoring in history, he graduated from college *cum laude* and taught school for two years before being drafted for World War II.

Mrs. Hines was the oldest of five children born to a rather prosperous farmer in rural North Carolina. Her family was extremely close-knit, and education and religion were stressed as the foundations for a good life. Mrs. Hines attended State College, where she met Mr. Hines at a football game. They dated rather infrequently, both as students and later, as young teachers. With the outbreak of the war, Mrs. Hines went to Washington, D.C., where she worked. She continued to correspond with Mr. Hines and accepted the engagement ring he sent her from overseas. Upon his return, they were married, and returned to Raleigh to make their home.

Unable to find steady employment in a well-paying field, Mr. Hines accepted various odd jobs at the Veterans Hospital. To supplement the income, Mrs. Hines became a secretary.

Eventually, Mr. Hines became a postal employee and Mrs. Hines stopped working to await the arrival of their first child. They began making payments on an old, two-story house in a quiet, residential black section of town.

Daughter Jane was born at mid-century; then Mrs. Hines returned to work. The baby was cared for during the day by an elderly couple who lived across the street. At age two, Jane got her first taste of school, when she entered the neighborhood nursery.

During the next eight years, the young couple worked very hard. Meanwhile, Mrs. Hines had secured a Master's degree and was again working as a teacher. The couple had paid off the mortgage on the house and owned all of their dilapidated furniture and second-hand appliances.

At just about this time, one of Mr. Hines' foster brothers died and a seven-year-old son was left homeless. The Hineses decided to adopt the child as their own — and Peter became a full-fledged member of the family. Parents and childrem seemingly enjoyed the enlarged family set-up and soon began clamoring for another sibling. Through a process of "familial consensus," they decided to adopt a little girl who really needed a family. The result was the addition of Beverly, who was then four years old. Both child and family evidently made the transition quite easily, as there is no outward evidence of discrimination on the family's part, or insecurity on the child's part. Beverly is treated as any other "baby of the family."

All of the Hines children were brought up in an upwardly mobile family group. Each child was given music lessons for the instrument of his or her choice, and each was sent to dance school for at least four years. Explains Mrs. Hines, "We wanted to give them as much culture and refinement as we could. Besides, any musical endeavor is worth encouraging."

There is a strong emphasis on education in the Hines family. The bookshelves overflow with five sets of encyclopedias, assorted textbooks, and remnants of numerous Book Club memberships. Interestingly enough, all three children are avid readers. Jane has proved herself to be a very intelligent young lady and is remembered to have "practically read herself blind as a child." The most enthusiastic reader is Peter, often referred to as the family egghead. An aspiring young scientist, he reads just about anything he can get his hands on. Like Jane, he has been an Honor Roll student all through high school. Beverly, on the other hand, has trouble in school. Math is her personal cross — whether old or new. "She just can't seem to buckle down in school," says her father. Nevertheless, Beverly is faithful to her books and brings home at least two books a week from the school library. Last summer she begged for membership in the Children's Book Club and most of her present allowance is spent on books.

Another major influence in this family's life is the church. Mr. Hines is a Baptist deacon and staunch church-goer. His wife was born and bred a Methodist and has remained true to her native demonination. Characteristically, each of the children expressed a preference for "Daddy's Church" while they were young. Now, Jane goes to church with her mother, Peter attends a Baptist Church (different from his father's) where he plays the organ, and Beverly attends the Lutheran Church on the corner. "We don't care where they go to church," remarked Mr. Hines, "just as long as they go."

The character of the Hineses' neighborhood underwent a rapid transition as the older residents died. Their single-family homes were converted into low-rent apartments, and those neighbors who could afford it began to migrate to the suburbs. The Hineses talked it over and decided they, too, should move, for Beverly was picking up traits that Mrs. Hines did not particularly appreciate. Thus they built a home in a previously undeveloped suburb. This section has now developed into one of the more prosperous black sections of the metropolitan area. The Hineses are quite content with this neighborhood and feel that it provides the "proper atmosphere" for rearing children. They do not anticipate moving again. When asked what he liked most about the neighborhood, Mr. Hines replied, "The neighborhood is nice, clean, and secure. It is easily accessible to churches, schools, and shopping centers. It is spread out enough to give you some sense of freedom, and yet, compact enough to ensure a sence of community."

The Hineses are quite active in civic affairs. Mr. Hines is president of the Community Club and works hard to establish solidarity among the neighbors. He takes an active interest in the welfare of the children and, despite his age, coaches a Little League baseball team. He is president of the Parent-Teacher Association at Beverly's school and works actively in several civic and civil rights groups. Mrs. Hines works basically with professional organizations — especially those dedicated to bettering educational opportunities for blacks. She is the voting ward representative for her area and spends much time encouraging others to vote and to participate in citizenship activities. Though their interests are diverse, the Hineses express a mutual respect for each other's independence. They do believe that their activities stem from like concerns and that they are working for the same types of goals.

The Hineses are a rather close-knit family, although individuality is important to them. The family rarely eats together during the week, but seldom does a member eat entirely alone. The varied schedules usually allow for at least two people to sit down at the table together. However, weekends are different. For Saturday breakfasts, Mrs. Hines eats with the children, and everyone waits for Mr. Hines to join them at Saturday's impromptu dinner. Sunday breakfast is the meal the family considers most important, as they all gather around for prayers before eating. Sunday dinner is a major production and everyone is involved, either in its preparation, or in cleaning up afterwards.

The parents do not indulge their children's whims. However, they see to it that the children have everything they need — and more. Thrift and industry are necessary components of each child's upbringing. Each child was encouraged at a very young age (six to nine) to get a weekend or part-time job, and to use his or her earnings to buy some of the things he or she wanted. Each of the Hines children receives an allowance, with a starting weekly rate doled out at age five that increased regularly until age eighteen. Commenting on this somewhat meager allowance, Mr. Hines said, "It lets them know that Mom and Dad are willing to help financially, but it gives them the incentive to get out and do for themselves." Apparently this logic has been pretty effective, as all of the children earn their own spending change, as well as contribute substantial amounts to their savings accounts.

The Hines children are fiercely critical, and yet extremely tolerant and extremely protective of each other. They class themselves as a tough lot to beat, saying, "We are stubborn like Daddy and independent like Mom — and that's quite a combination!" Though they all evaluate themselves as being somewhat shy and reserved, they come across as being very self-confident and quite capable of any task they may undertake. They are competitive among themselves and their peers, but not jealously or covetously so. "Competition," says Jane, "keeps you from stagnation. It lets you know that no matter how good you are, you can always be better."

The Hines children have an enormous respect for their parents and a deep appreciation for the way in which they have been brought up. Commented Jane, "Mom and Dad instilled us with certain basic values and then allowed us to apply these values to our individual personalities. We may express ourselves differently, but I don't think any of us will ever really depart from our upbringing. We know and respect the difference between right and wrong."

When asked if there was a generation gap within the family, Peter replied, "Only when it comes to money. Pops still doesn't realize that things cost more now than they did in the twelfth century when he was growing up. Other than that, he is much more liberal and eager to understand than are the parents of most of my friends." Mrs. Hines' response to inquiries about a generation gap was this: "I want to understand my kids, so I ask and listen to find out what they are thinking and why." She feels that she is able to communicate well with her children as a result of this effort. "If there is a gap in this family, it is more likely to be between me and my husband," she laughs. The children agreed. Beverly summed up the whole question by saying "They are pretty hep for old folks!"

Father — Mr. Hines, over fifty — is a rather easygoing man. He is a big man (200 pounds), with a rather stern countenance, but a quick smile. He is devoted to his family and to fulfilling what he considers to be the "fatherly" role. He respects and admires his wife's independence, commenting that he could not have married a "tie-me-down" type woman.

Recalling his boyhood poverty and deprivation, Mr. Hines is determined that his family have the basics for a good start in life. These basics include: a good home (food, shelter, clothing), and education, good principles and love. He is a concerned father who disciplines his children with a heavy hand and admits that he often listens after he strikes. He takes an active interest in whatever the children are doing, always joining or organizing a corresponding parent group. He shows his affection for both his wife and children mostly in play, admitting that it is hard for him to be affectionate in the conventional ways.

Mr. Hines is indisputedly the man of the house, and the final authority — but not, he insists, the authoritarian. "We are a family," he says," not a military company."

Mother — Mrs. Hines, middle-aged — is a typical, atypical mother. She is bouncy, yet often fatigued; fussy, but understanding; older in age, but young in actions; quiet spoken, but quick to make her opinions known. She is rather short and about fifteen pounds overweight (a nervous eater she says.). She suffers with every conceivable ache and pain (a typical hypochondriac her husband says), yet lets nothing slow her down.

During the course of the interview, her face changed back and forth from school teacher and disciplinarian to loving, compassionate mother. While acknowledging obstacles and personal limitations, Mrs. Hines firmly believes "you can do anything you put your mind to doing" and hopes she has instilled this feeling in her children.

"My husband and I worked long and hard to give these kids the opportunities we never had. We are not going to force them to take advantage of their chances but if they choose to do so, they will have enough stamina and love behind them to make the best of any opportunity." So said, and apparently, so believes, Mrs. Hines.

Daughter Number One — Jane — is a coed at the University of North Carolina, where she is enrolled in the pre-medical program. She hopes to be a hematologist. An honor student throughout high school, Jane excelled in many things and participated in practically everything. She is a good musician, being an accomplished pianist and a "half-cocked" flutist. She is a member of the Modern Dance Troupe at school and has been (to her parents' dismay) excessively active in the Black Student Movement. She does not consider herself a militant, but she does believe in asserting the rights of the individual.

Jane is easygoing and appears, at first glance, quite reserved. She can, however, get very excited over some idea she is interested in and often finds herself thrust into leadership roles. She says of herself, "I am an incurably, romantic, realistic idealist. I know what the world is really like and I accept it. At the same time, I want it to be better, and deep down inside, I believe someday it will be." "I am," she says reflectively, "the product of my parents' love, wisdom, and being."

Son — Peter, a teenager — is a big man on his high school campus. President of his senior class, he is both an athlete and a scholar. Particularly interested in physics ("I get it from Mom," he grins), he hopes to major in bio-physics at Cornell, MIT, or Harvard. He is a very outgoing young man with both an easy smile and a quick temper. He is incredibly honest, hates phonies, and will go to any end for a friend. Very industrious, he works at a gas station on weekend days. plays with a jazz band on weekend nights, and is church organist on Sunday morning. When asked which of his parents influenced him most, he replied, "I guess Dad had the most influence on my manliness, while Mom influenced my being the kind of man I am."

Daughter Number Two — Beverly — is a perky, button-nosed miss. Often called "The Brat" by her brother and sister, she is the most precocious of the Hines children. Although she is active in many groups, she confesses that she often gets very lonely. Unlike her siblings, Beverly has an acute dislike for being alone and often feels compelled to seek out friends for company.

She idolizes her older sister and brother and adores her

parents. When asked what her family was like, Beverly said, "They are like my family — You know, like you wouldn't want to belong to any other family but them." An engaging little girl, Beverly has the amazing ability of switching instantly from "Little Imp" to "Little Angel." Extemely outgoing around adults, she is somewhat timid of new friends her own age. An avid member of the "Now Generation," Beverly thinks that all in all, her family is a real "groove."

Upon visiting the Hines family, I was ushered into the den of a very modern, well-furnished home. The atmosphere was decidedly informal and congenial. The family was most cooperative and I was able to interview each member of the family individually.

In this stable, middle-income family, the influence pattern is obviously equalitarian and the system of family decision-making is democratic. All members of the family concurred that theirs is a stable and happy unit. From observation, this interviewer must agree with their consensus.

THE SCHOOL MARM AND THE POSTAL WORKER
Judy Mesinger

Hillsborough, New York, population 72,000, is a suburb of New York City. Fore more than fifty years, this four-square-mile city has been bifurcated along black and white racial lines by the railroad tracks. Though economic status and racial identity overlap to a great extent, the wealthy reside in the northern part of the city and the poor whites reside in the southern part. Elementary and junior high schools are also populated on this basis, while the city's sole high school serves all youth from ninth to twelfth grades.

Driving up the Phillipses' block on Hillsborough's south side at 9:00 a.m., I noticed the neatly kept old houses. Considering the morning hour and the fact that the children were on vacation, the street was very quiet.

Mrs. Phillips had just come back from driving her husband to work and was talking on the telephone when I knocked on her door. She hurriedly excused herself from the phone and ushered me in through the foyer and a well-equipped modern kitchen to their dining room, where she offered me a cup of coffee.

The Phillipses are a black family headed by Andrew and Sara, ages sixty and forty-six respectively. They have been married for twenty years and have two daughters, Carol, age eighteen, and Shirley, age sixteen.

While Mr. Phillips was born in Pennsylvania and Mrs. Phillips in South Carolina, both their daughters have been life-long residents of Hillsborough. Before coming to Hillsborough to live, both husband and wife lived in Virginia. Mr. Phillips has been a resident of Hillsborough for thirty years, though Mrs. Phillips has lived there for only twenty years.

Currently a freshman at Wellesley College (Wellesley, Massachusetts), Carol spends about four months out of the year at home. All information concerning Carol is based on vacations spent at home during the academic year. Her younger sister is a junior in Hillsborough high school. Mr. Phillips has completed three years of college and Mrs. Phillips has her Bachelor of Arts degree plus an additional thirty-nine credit hours towards a doctoral degree.

Andrew Phillips is a postal clerk at the local post office, selling stamps and processing mail. Before becoming an employee of the post office, he was an upholsterer. When the couple married, he switched from this trade to his present job because of better salary conditions. He still keeps the latter up as a hobby and has made all the furniture for his house. When he retires, his wife said he intends to return to upholstering on a full-time basis.

Sara Phillips teaches sixth grade in a south side elementary school and has done so for the past five years. Even though she teaches in the same school her daughters attended, and would have been able to be home for lunch with them, she did not work when her daughters were younger because she did not want to be away from home. Before coming to Hillsborough with one of her sisters, she taught elementary school for more than three years in Virginia.

Together, Andrew and Sara Phillips gross a yearly income that is slightly above the national median. Mrs. Phillips has contributed slightly more to the family income than her husband.

Both Mr. and Mrs. Phillips are Presbyterians. When they switched churches several years ago, Mr. and Mrs. Phillips made individual choices. Nevertheless, they chose the same church. Both girls attended the same church regularly each Sunday with their parents. Before services, Mrs. Phillips teaches Sunday school and during the services, Mr. Phillips sings in the choir. In addition to these church activities, the senior Phillipses are members of a play reading group and The Couples Club, and Mrs. Phillips participates in The Women's Society. Meetings of these church-affiliated organizations require Mr. and Mrs. Phillips to be at their church at least one day a week other than Sunday.

Mrs. Phillips classified her family as "close." She felt there should be something more if one were going to label a family "real close."

Carol and Shirley, their daughters, never got into trouble with the police and did very well in school. Their mother also reported that she and her husband share the responsibility of disciplining the girls. Mrs. Phillips, however, admitted that she played a slightly bigger role in this area because she was home more often.

The Phillipses dine together every night at 6:00 p.m. except on Sundays, when they eat at 5:00 p.m. During the normal school year, the entire family has lunch separately. Carol is the only one to eat lunch at home; the other three family members eat at their places of work. Mr. and Mrs. Phillips have breakfast together and Shirley has hers about half an hour later with her sister, if the latter is home.

Mrs. Phillips characterized Sundays at her home as quiet days. The whole family has breakfast together at 8:00 a.m., or shortly after. Mrs. Phillips then leaves to teach church school while her daughters clean up. Before they go to church, they join their father to read the newspaper. The entire family, as noted before, attends services and Mr. Phillips sings in the choir. They return home for a noon dinner, after which the girls wash the dishes. By approximately 2:00 p.m. the girls are studying. After lunch, Mrs. Phillips naps or sometimes corrects papers. Mr. Phillips spends his afternoon constructing furniture or making repairs about the house. After a 5:00 p.m. supper for the whole family, the parents frequently visit friends or relatives. Meanwhile, Carol studies and Shirley goes to a youth group meeting until 9:00 p.m. Upon returning, the latter studies until 11:00 and both sisters retire a half hour later. Despite the fact that both children have desks in their rooms, Shirley studies at the dining room table, usually along with her sister. Mr. and Mrs. Phillips also return home at 9:00 and go to sleep an hour later.

On weekdays, such as Tuesday, Mr. and Mrs. Phillips have breakfast at 7:00 a.m. By that time Carol and Shirley are getting up. While the girls are eating breakfast, Mrs. Phillips leaves to drive to her elementary school, which she does not normally leave until 3:30 p.m., or later. Mr. Phillips, on the other hand, works until 5:00 p.m. They both eat lunch, which they have brought from home, at approximately noon. Shirley is at school by 8:45 a.m. and is finished with her classes by 2:45 p.m. From then on until 5:30 she usually attends meetings of various school organizations. Carol, on the other hand, spends most of her morning studying until lunch time. In the afternoon she visits friends or travels to New York City. When Mrs. Phillips does not have her 4:00 to 6:00 p.m. university course (it usually meets on Wednesdays), she picks her husband up from work, after an hour and a half of making lesson plans. Mrs. Phillips then spends the next hour preparing dinner. Usually, their parents have a meeting, so the girls will wash the dishes. Carol and Shirley spend the rest of the night studying, going to sleep about 11:00 or 11:30. The elder Phillipses are generally in bed an hour before the girls.

The Phillipses seem to be active in school affairs. They attend PTA meetings regularly and go to parent-teacher conferences. No teacher or school official has ever visited their household, although Shirley's math teacher called Mrs. Phillips once because of poor performance on her daughter's part.

Until recently, Mrs. Phillips has been satisfied with the education of her daughters in Hillsborough schools. Now, with the elimination of counselors in the elementary schools, where they are needed most urgently, Mrs. Phillips believes more youth will "turn bad" and never complete high school. Furthermore, she thinks classes are too large and floating classes are not a good idea for elementary-school-aged children. In elementary schools more help is needed so that the children don't fall behind in their work to the point where they can't ever catch up, Mrs. Phillips believes. Moreover, she would have supervisors and longer planning periods, so that teachers would not have to take too much work home with them.

Mrs. Phillips described herself and her husband as being very interested in their daughters' futures. Having attended Metropolitan School of Music for five years on Saturdays, Carol entered Wellesley College as a piano major this past fall. She is doing very well, according to her mother, but does not find it challenging enough. Carol has a new interest in psychology and her mother has encouraged her to pursue it.

However, she would like Carol to continue with music, which could serve as a hobby. Mrs. Phillips said she'd be delighted if her older daughter decides to become a school psychologist. Considering Shirley's talent with her hands, as well as her artistic and sewing ability, the Phillipses could see their younger daughter becoming a decorator. Furthermore, it is expected that some day both girls will marry.

Mrs. Phillips has mixed feelings about her neighborhood, which is comprised of a majority of middle-class and many working-class people. She is dissatisfied with the neighborhood, and the nearby school in which she teaches because of some juvenile behavior problems. She stresses the need for more parental supervision. Otherwise, any amount of cohesiveness in a neighborhood will be insufficient when it is a problem of coping with occasional juvenile misbehavior. Though she is most troubled by these discipline problems, and would like to change them, she thinks the people are the best thing about her neighborhood and knows 150 to 175 of them. The Phillipses' immediate neighborhood of two blocks has formed a block association, which has increased this family's satisfaction. Within this association, caring about one's neighbors has greatly increased, and its members can talk about common problems of the area. Police law enforcement is considered as just by Mrs. Phillips. She would like to see, however, more police protection. Generally, Mrs. Phillips sees the area as average, tending to safe.

The Phillipses have never considered moving away from their neighborhood, but Mrs. Phillips would like a larger house within this section. They have been living in their present seven-room house for about ten years. The Phillipses own their single-family home. Both daughters have their own bedrooms and the parents occupy the third one. There is also one kitchen, living room, dining room, and basement. They own a radio, television, and two telephones. They also have a stereo and a piano.

If she ever needed help, Mrs. Phillips would ask one of her two sisters and their husbands or her neighbor across the street. (Her sisters were the deciding factor in her move to Hillsborough). She sees each of the families several times during the course of a week. Though she has known her sisters all her life, she has known the neighbor only thirteen years.

The decision-making pattern in this household is largely equalitarian. Noncrisis decisions are shared equally by mother and father, with two major exceptions. First of all, Mrs. Phillips makes all the decisions traditionally connected with her role as mother and wife. She plans the meals and cooks them and has decided on the number of children to have. Now that her daughters are older, she will no longer take care of them all of the time when they are sick because they are more capable now of doing it themselves. Since she works it means both parents can now share the responsibility. The fact that she teaches also means that parent-teacher conferences are no longer her sole responsibility; she shares them with her husband. With older daughters, her duty to help them decide what to wear has been replaced by the girls consulting each other. The second exception is Mr. Phillips' sole power to choose his occupation.

This family actively participates in numerous and varied organizations. Mr. Phillips is in a play-reading group; he is a PTA and block association member as well as belonging to church groups. Mrs. Phillips participates in a church-connected organization too. In addition, she belongs to the PTA, Nursery Association for the Education of Young Children, Foreign Student Exchange Committee, and the County Chapter of the Association of the Study of Black Life and History. During her freshman year at college, Carol has become a member of the choir and the Black Students Organization. Shirley belongs to the Girl Scouts, Foreign Student Exchange Committee, a youth group at the YWCA, and Future Teachers of America.

Consequently, it appears from the above discussion that the Phillipses are a stable, middle-class, black family living in a combined middle-class, working-class black neighborhood. The stability of their family is increased by regular church attendance and dinner-time activities. More important, perhaps, familial stability is enhanced by the respect accorded each member, especially in making decisions. For example, when a daughter must make a decision regarding her future, she discusses the matter with her parents and vice versa; when a church had to be selected, Mr. and Mrs. Phillips chose independently. As Mrs. Phillips has stated, she could have never forced her husband to compromise on a matter of deep personal concern to him.

Mr. Phillips' position as a postal worker seems to indicate that his education has not fully paid off. Mrs. Phillips' decision to go back to work after her children were older seems to represent a desire to increase the family's socioeconomic status within society's main stratification system and thereby obtain the additional material benefits which accompany financial well-being.

It appears, moreover, that Mr. and Mrs. Phillips have been very effective in their roles of socializing their children. This aspect of socialization, when added to the factors of an increasingly open society for mobility, available familial resources, and the children's ability, indicate that Carol and Shirley should be able to achieve their goals.

Though the Phillipses are not an extended family as commonly defined, they maintain a very close relationship with Mrs. Phillips' two sisters and their families.

DOING WHAT COMES NATURALLY
Karin Caruso

Mr. and Mrs. Emerson have been happily married for fifteen years. Samuel is thirty-seven and his wife, June, is thirty-five. They live with their two children in a middle-class residential area. Samuel, Jr. is thirteen and in the eighth grade. His ten-year-old sister, Sarah, is in the fifth grade. Mr. and Mrs. Emerson are originally from New England but they have lived in the Upstate New York area since their marriage.

Both Mr. and Mrs. Emerson graduated from college. Mrs. Emerson is an elementary school teacher and her husband, who went on for his master's, is the head of the science department in a public high school. Mr. and Mrs. Emerson are employed by the same public school system and have excellent attendance records.

Mrs. Emerson was happy that family illnesses were minimal this past year. Her husband suffered no illness that was serious enough to confine him to bed. She, however, spent about one week in bed while recovering from a minor operation. Since the children have been inoculated or have had all of the usual childhood diseases, their only illnesses were minor viruses and the common cold. Mrs. Emerson considered this fortunate since she is more likely to stay home from work and care for the children if illness strikes.

The family's religious preference is Methodist. They do not regularly attend church, but are somewhat "holiday goers." However, they feel that this is no measure of their belief. Their children attend Sunday School moderately during the winter, but never on a beautiful summer day. And, the parents are members of the Church Couples Club.

The family is very close, with both parents sharing disciplinary responsibilities. The children are assigned few chores beyond keeping their bedrooms picked up. Spring cleaning and any outside work is usually done by the family as a whole. The children are responsible enough to decide when they should do their own homework. This is done at their respective desks in their bedrooms while sometimes listening to a radio in the background. The parents offer assistance equally. Mrs. Emerson helps with English, while her husband's assistance is concentrated in science and mathematics. She said laughingly, that if it was a foreign language, neither of them would be of much help.

A typical day would start with the mother and father waking at six-thirty. The children are awakened at seven a.m. Mrs. Emerson helps her daughter decide what to wear; but Samuel, Jr. makes his own decisions. By seven-thirty, the family is ready to sit down to a big breakfast. Mr. Emerson is off to work by eight o'clock, and the children catch separate school buses at about eight-thirty. The mother leaves for school at eight-forty since she takes a more direct route, which gives her plenty of time to see everyone off safely.

The family members eat lunch at their designated times while in their respective schools. Since the children ride home by bus, Mrs. Emerson arrives home before them at about three-fifteen. Samuel, Jr. and Sarah bid their friends on their buses good-bye between three-thirty and three-forty, as their mother awaits them with an afternoon snack.

The children may watch color television, or if there is dissent over the program, Samuel, Jr. usually wanders to the set in the recreation room. If it's nice outside, the children may go and play with their friends in the neighborhood. But if the weather is bad, their friends are invited into the playroom in the basement — possibly for a game of ping pong. Once a week Sarah has her Girl Scout meeting and biweekly Samuel, Jr. meets with his Boy Scout troop.

Mr. Emerson rarely arrives home before four-fifteen. His first move is towards his favorite chair with the *New York Times* in one hand. He may put on the stereo to create a relaxing background. Since he and his wife both work, it is not unusual for him to lend a hand to his wife in picking up the house. He and his wife are capable of discussing the headlines, but afternoon conversation is generally more related to the events of the day and issues which they are immediately affected by or responsible for.

The children may or may not come in before dinner to start their homework. Dinner is usually served around "sixish," but changes in time for convenience' sake are easily made. Mrs. Emerson does most of the cooking and Sarah often likes to help. The meal is planned by mother with welcomed suggestions from her husband and her children alike. The dinner conversation attempts to include everyone and may range from a movie, to a family member's new bicycle, to plans for the weekend or summer vacation. After dinner, Sarah clears the table and Samuel, Jr. disposes of the left-overs while Mrs. Emerson stacks the dishwasher.

By seven o'clock, one may find the Emerson family gathered around the television or each member about his or her own activity. Mr. and Mrs. Emerson may correct papers and draw up lesson plans. The children may do their homework or they may play a game such as Monopoly. School activities are usually taken in by the family.

So pass the hours between seven and ten, and then it is the children's bed time. Time for bed is not an unalterable declaration but may vary with the evening's activities. Therefore, the children rarely contest their time for sleep. Mr. and Mrs. Emerson enjoy being alone together. They usually watch the eleven o'clock news. They may watch a movie, listen to records, or converse. Working hours require that the lights in the Emerson home are extinguished by twelve.

Both Saturdays and Sundays are family days. The family sleeps until nine and Mr. Emerson often makes the breakfast to give his wife a rest. On occasion, the children may be up and out playing before the parents awake, leaving a note to say where they could be found. The children may attend Sunday School at ten or the family may go to church at eleven. Sunday is a day for relaxing. Their activity is rarely predictable for any hour of the day. In the winter, the family frequently goes skiing for the day. If not skiing, they may go sledding around the neighborhood. Summer may find them working in the yard. The children may play with friends or go swimming at the pool club to which the family belongs.

The family may go to visit friends or relatives. If they remain home, a big meal is served at three o'clock. And the evening snack is often accompanied by friends or relatives invited for coffee and a chat.

Mr. and Mrs. Emerson each chose their professions before marriage. Mrs. Emerson does not work during the summer. She spends her summer months taking care of her children and relaxing. She catches up on some of the reading she had wanted to pursue during the school year. Her husband, as the head of the science department, makes about one and one-half times what she earns. He remains employed by the school board during the months of June and July, when he helps organize the high school curriculum for the coming year. This summer job adds about 20 percent more to his yearly income. The combined family income contributes to comfortable but not luxury living. They anticipate that their children will attend college. Neither parent has attempted to influence their children's choice of adult occupation, at such as early age. Samuel, Jr. is presently enthralled with science and would like to go into research, while Sarah wants to become just like her mother and be an elementary school teacher.

If a parent-teacher conference was called, Mrs. Emerson would try to schedule it at a time when she and her husband could attend. Teachers frequent the Emerson home for meetings and social occasions, but not to discuss Samuel's or Sarah's school problems. The children are quite bright; and they have no problems either academic or social in school.

Unlike household decisions made on an equal basis, the parents make political decisions on an individual basis. As school teachers, the parents are members of the PTA and a teacher's union. Mrs. Emerson belongs to the Women's League and her husband is a member of a local men's club.

The Emersons are close to seven families in their neighborhood. However, when they entertain, more than seven neighborhood names will appear on their guest list, as friends. It is a racially mixed neighborhood, with a solid midle-class status. Because of compatible incomes and interests, there is no noticeable racial segragation. The Emersons entertain and are invited in the homes of neighbors. The Emersons enjoy their home environment and have no desire to move.

Their eight-room house, which they own, is a four-bedroom semi-colonial. It has all the conveniences of any other middle-class home. What Mrs. Emerson enjoys most about her neighborhood is the opportunity for privacy as a family unit, complemented by healthy and friendly surroundings. The Emersons are self-sufficient, but could easily turn to their next-door neighbors for assistance. They are close friends with the engineer and his family who moved next door five years ago. And, if Mrs. Emerson had any power to change her neighborhood, her request would be to stop building more houses and to put an embargo on developers who cut down all of "my trees."

Mr. and Mrs. Emerson are not exactly self-integrators. They were not the first black family to move into the neighborhood. Mrs. Emerson said that the neighborhood had no "noticeable" racism. However, she feels some of the same patronizing attitudes — "Did the school principal remember my name, among all those people at the PTA meeting ... because of what we are?" — that many black suburban families experience. The Emerson family also leans toward social, fraternal, and professional clubs, and do not ally themselves with social action organizations.

The equalitatian locus of family power in child-rearing, recreation, and other roles is probably due to the fact that both parents work, although Mrs. Emerson seems to have slightly more influence on the children's plans than does the father. This may be partially attributed to the fact that she spends more time with the children during the summer.

The Emerson family is stable, is apparently a more well-adjusted family than most. Mr. and Mrs. Emerson both came from stable middle-class families; and they look forward with optimism for a satisfactory future for their children.

Because of their backgrounds, Mr. and Mrs. Emerson both had the opportunity to attend college. Both parents chose the teaching profession because they realized that it was the one most accessible to them as blacks at that time. Mr. Emerson attained a higher level of education than his wife.

Samuel and June Emerson were married at ages twenty-two and twenty respectively. Mrs. Emerson had both of her children before the age of twenty-five. Her "null" fertility from age twenty-five on supports the finding that college-educated black women have a low fertility rate. This is especially true of black teachers.

Mr. and Mrs. Emerson have gained more than a middle-class socioeconomic status. They have also gained and maintained a happy and healthy family.

6 WORKING–CLASS INNOVATORS

The family patterns of six working-class black kinship units are presented in this chapter. Five of the six families are two-parent, although one family has a very sick father who is not expected to live long. Two of the six families are second marriages; death and divorce contributed to the disintegration of the first marriage. The wife is a high school graduate in two of the families, and probably a high-school dropout in the other four cases, although education is not mentioned in two cases. The husband is a high school dropout, having completed only the tenth or eleventh grades, in three cases, and an elementary school dropout in one case. Mention of the husband's education was omitted in two cases but is believed to be at the high school level or less. Four of the families live in inner-city black ghettoes and two live outside cities — one in a suburb and the other in an isolated rural area.

The Chandler household consists of husband, wife, and four children, together with the mother's sister and the wife of one of the sons. The father is a self-employed junkyard dealer and the mother, a part-time receptionist. Ms. Eaton has four children derived from two marriages. Mr. Eaton, a sandblaster, died from a disease connected with his occupation. His widow works as a case aide for the school system. The Brown family is a six-child family. The wife and mother is a nurse's aide and the husband's occupation is not given. The Farmers have two children; the father is hospitalized and not expected to live much longer. When employed, he was a semiskilled worker; the mother is a cook. The Wilson household is a two-parent family that includes seven children and one grandchild. The father is a janitor and the mother, a nurse's aide. The Henderson family lives in public housing and has two children, one an adult offspring of a first marriage that was dissolved because of the death of the wife, and the other a young child from the present marriage. The mother does not work outside the home.

In five of the six working-class households, the mother is in the labor force. In all households where there is a father present, he is employed, or was employed in the case of the hospitalized man. The wages of the offspring also are significant in family finances in five of the six households. These families exist on annual incomes that range from above the official poverty line up to the national median.

POOLING EARNINGS FOR FAMILY SURVIVAL
Alan Haymon

The Chandler family lives in a two-family home in Chicago, Illinois. The Chandlers are in the process of paying off the mortgage on their modest house. The exterior of the 13-room house (which includes a finished attic) is in need of painting and minor repair. The home is furnished with attractive but old furniture. Several televisions (some color) and a pair of stereo systems are present, as well as many modern appliances. In essence, the interior of the home is immaculate. The driveway is laced with cars (the Chandler family owns three of varying vintage, including a 5-year old Buick, the newest of the collection). Mrs. Chandler was quite cooperative and anxious to show and discuss their home and several "special" pieces of furniture. The dining room table received particular mention as the first piece of furniture purchased for the house about 20 years ago. Mrs. Chandler, a rather soft-spoken miniature woman in her early fifties, exhibits obvious pride and happiness when speaking of her home. The cleanliness of the household is a result of her personal efforts.

When asked, Mrs. Chandler described the members of the household as being very close to each other and seldom at odds with each other. Although rather quiet, Mrs. Chandler obviously commands the respect of the children as evidenced by how readily they respond to her commands. The youngest son, James, was asked to empty the garbage while I was present and he heeded this request immediately. When asked about obedience, Mrs. Chandler said, "I've raised four boys and none of them have ever talked back to me, not even once."

Mr. Chandler's only participation in the conversation was to greet me with a resounding "hello and make yourself at home" upon my arrival. A rather muscular man in his mid-fifties, Mr. Chandler has an imposing voice which also commands respect. He clearly is *the* "man of the house."

Mr. and Mrs. Chandler have been married for 34 years. They have had what Mrs. Chandler described as "many lean years." Now, however, Mr. Chandler owns and operates a junk and scrap yard which provides the family with a livable income but not much for luxury living. Mrs. Chandler works part-time as a receptionist in an office and earns about half as much as her husband. The family would experience great difficulty if it had to exist on the single income of the mother or the father. Even their combined income is less than the national median.

The Chandlers have four sons ranging in age from 17 to 33. They all live at home. Also living in the household is the oldest son's wife and Mrs. Chandler's younger sister. Mrs. Chandler's sister has been living with the Chandlers for almost 10 years, ever since the death of her husband.

All of the Chandler offspring, except the youngest who attends high school, work full-time. The oldest son has been married for six years and is an auto mechanic for a local car dealer. His earnings are about the same as his father's. The wife of the oldest son works part-time as a secretary in a physician's office and earns about as much as her mother-in-law. The second son works for his father at the junk yard and performs a variety of odd tasks, including driving the tow truck to pick up scrap autos. The third son is employed full-time as a maintenance man for the Public School System.

When asked about the family's combined earnings, Mrs. Chandler's quick reply was this: "My sons work and earn their own money, they live with me and pay no rent because we ask for none. More often than not on their own they offer money for the weekly groceries and the mortgage payments. I usually take it and occasionally I don't. But if we were in trouble, we would simply all pool our earnings to survive." She said that her sister gets a check from the government, and "if it's not enough we don't worry." Thus the Chandler household is comprised of eight members. All of the sons were born and raised in Chicago, except the oldest, who was born in Alabama as were Mr. and Mrs. Chandler. The family has lived in Chicago for about 31 years. They report that they came to Chicago because they had been told work could be found there.

Mr. and Mrs. Chandler met in Alabama and married over 30 years ago. They both came from rather poor families, although Mrs. Chandler states that her family owned the house and land they lived on. Mr. Chandler's family was less fortunate and survived primarily by farming. Neither set of parents received much education. However, Mrs. Chandler was the third of 11 children. She said, "My parents were much quicker to discipline our kids." She described the folks as the kind who believe in kids behaving and knowing right from wrong.

Clearly Mrs. Chandler was the undisputed spokesperson for her contemporary family. But contrary to what one might expect, Mrs. Chandler said that her husband administers all punishments and acts as household disciplinarian. Mrs. Chandler's role in the discipline process is to single out who has to be punished and to indicate why. When asked if she and her husband usually concur about such matters, she said, "yes."

All of the Chandler boys, except the second, completed (or are in the process of completing) high school. Mrs. Chandler said that the second child "has been mentally deficient since birth and wasn't able to finish school." He attended the local public school and took classes for slower students, but did not receive any special education services. When asked why he never attended a special school, Mrs. Chandler stated that "We didn't think he needed any special school. He can learn like anyone else; it just takes him a while longer. Right now he's learned how to help my husband run the scrap yard." The only individual in the household who attended college is the wife of the oldest son; she quit after two years. The oldest son went to mechanics school upon graduating from school.

Mrs. Chandler states that all of her sons "had done fair in school," and that the last child now in high school is "doing O.K." For this reason she never had to stipulate a specific time for him or others to do homework. She tries to attend local Parent-Teacher Association meetings and has always done so in the past. Mrs. Chandler believes that you cannot force education on anyone. She said, "I have always insisted that my kids graduate from high school and go on if they so desire. I wanted very much for one or more of my sons to go on to college and thought that my oldest son would, because he is so smart, but he didn't want to. Now, the youngest is the only child left in school, and he's just not cut out for college. I'd be satisfied seeing him become a foreman or something."

Mrs. Chandler was quick to say that none of her boys had ever been in any trouble with the law. But later in the interview she revealed that the third son had once gotten into a bit of trouble. He had been driving a friend home when he was in high school; the friend pulled out a gun and shot at someone they passed on the street. No one was injured and charges against her son were dropped before the case ever got to court. Mrs. Chandler more or less dismissed the incident as being very unintentional on her son's part.

Mrs. Chandler said that she and her husband's main goal in raising their children was to "teach them right from wrong" and instill in them a belief in God. She went on to say that they believed no matter what a person did for a living, as long as he did it well, then he was successful. Thus, they were very proud of their sons, whom they considered to be hard workers.

The members of the family belong to the Baptist Church. One son, however, joined the Methodist Church. Mrs. Chandler and her sister attend church weekly and often are accompanied by her oldest son and his wife. None of the other boys attended church very much, but, according to Mrs. Chandler, "they all have faith." She further mentioned that the entire family had attended church earlier in the year when Mr. Chandler suffered a mild stroke. Other than a stroke which immobilized Mrs. Chandler for a month earlier in the year, none of the family members has been very sick. Mrs. Chandler's sister has what was described as "a nervous condition."

The influence of religion on Mrs. Chandler's life was quite apparent. There was a large Bible on display in the living room and a large painting of Jesus Christ in the room. Mrs. Chandler states that attendance in Sunday school or church services was mandatory for all her sons when they were quite young, but that she could not and would not force them to attend as adults.

The Chandler family received morning and evening daily newspapers as well as a couple of magazines such as *Essence* and *Jet*. The family receives most news by watching television and reading the newspapers. Mrs. Chandler spends four to five hours a day watching television and talking on the telephone to friends. She watches the news daily, several soap operas, and an occasional detective story. Often, she views the television with her husband, who misses the news on weekdays because of his work. He watches late evening programs when he is not out on the street with the "fellas."

Televison is very much a part of the Chandler household. Mrs. Chandler and her sister watch several hours daily; the oldest son and his wife watch television together with family members two or three hours in the evening. The other three sons spend more of their evening hours "out in the streets." On Sundays the men in the household watch football, baseball, or whatever sport is on while Mrs. Chandler and her sister attend morning and evening church services. Sunday is the only time that all in the household eat dinner together. Except on Sundays, the family hardly ever eats together because of the work schedules. For example, the father and son who work in the junk yard often work until 7:00 p.m. and therefore miss the 5:00 p.m. dinner eaten by five members of the household. The oldest son works until after 6:00 p.m. and misses the 5:00 o'clock dinner hour also. Thus Sunday is still the only day they have a "family dinner," as Mrs. Chandler puts it. Though Mrs. Chandler insists that the family is quite close, seldom do they do anything together. She did make reference to trips the entire family used to make to Alabama 10 or more years ago to see their parents and grandparents. They do not take these together anymore.

Mrs. Chandler's sister helps her on weekends and she usually cooks the weekday meals since Mrs. Chandler works part-time. Her sister watches television often and occasionally sews.

Mrs. Chandler had mixed emotions about the neighborhood they live in. In general she seems moderately satisfied with it. She expresses a favorable opinion of her neighbors but said that she fears the rising crime rate. The neighborhood itself is predominantly black and best described as working class with a few lower-class residents. When asked about children in the community, she responded, "I can only talk about my own sons, and I know they are good. All I am sure of is that crime is rising fast in this area and I don't think the police really care that much one way or another about it." For this reason she describes the neighborhood as being of "average safety." Mrs. Chandler knows about a dozen or so other families in her neighborhood. She feels that in time of trouble she could depend on her neighbor two doors away whom she has known for 20 years. She also expresses great faith in her first cousin, whom she has known all her life, as well as another cousin who also lives in Chicago.

Mrs. Chandler said: "Now that we're almost finished paying for the house, the neighborhood has begun to go down. But we've worked hard to get this house and we're going to stay here. Besides, all the boys are grown up now, we don't need to move."

PERSEVERANCE AND SELF–HELP
Susan Kluver

Ms. Eaton has been a Providence, Rhode Island resident all of her life. One year after her second marriage, she and her husband bought a modest two-family home in the oldest, most stable section of the black community in Providence. Ms. Eaton was 25 at the time of her second marriage. She has been married before at the age of 18 and was divorced within two years. A son was born of this marriage. He now is 35 years old. Ms. Eaton referred only briefly to this former marriage and the problems of her oldest son, who had, as a teenager, been arrested for theft and who later as an adult was in and out of jail on weekends for nonsupport of his own wife and family.

Her memory, as well as her present emotional life, were invested in the family from her second marriage — a marriage which lasted for a decade and which ended 18 years ago due to the death of her husband. Mr. Eaton's death was related to his occupation. He had been a sand-blaster; when he developed a lung condition he changed his occupation to take up barbering. However, his lung condition was to lead to his death two years later.

Although Ms. Eaton had spoken acceptingly and affectionately of her eldest son, she described in greater detail her three children of the second marriage. Yvonne, her oldest daughter, had left home two years previously to join the Navy. Ms. Eaton spoke of Yvonne as a good student but without a strong interest, "still floundering." Ms. Eaton feels that Yvonne may be tiring of the service already after only a year. She had joined the service in order to travel and obtain different experiences. After completing the local high school, Yvonne had gone away for two years to Knoxville College in Tennessee and then had finished her college work closer to home at Rhode Island State. For a while after completing college, Yvonne worked in a boutique and lived in the downstairs apartment of

104

Ms. Eaton's home. Ms. Eaton thought that someday Yvonne might really be most fulfilled by opening up her own small boutique. She allowed as how Yvonne would need to conserve her money made in the service.

A son, Samuel, age 23, was born two years after the birth of Yvonne. Samuel, as all of her children, "loved school and didn't want to miss a day." Samuel, who had initially had aspirations to become a schoolteacher, was counseled away from this field by his mother at the time of his graduation from high school. Ms. Eaton, at that time, was concerned about the surplus of teachers. Samuel had attended two years of college at Oberlin College and had returned to complete his junior and senior years at the University of Rhode Island. Samuel was a strong support to his mother. He resided downstairs in the apartment the Yvonne had formerly used, worked part time to help earn money, and did the marketing during the week for the meals that he and his mother shared together. Samuel always had a part-time job during high school as well.

The youngest daughter, Ruth, was born two years after Samuel. She, like the other children, was "well behaved" and showed a "normal amount of adolescent rebelliousness." She was an excellent student in grammar school and wished to study medicine. By the time she completed high school, Ms. Eaton humorously noted, she didn't wish to continue with any schooling. "I had to think quickly," Ms. Eaton said, to help her daughter make a sound career decision. She recommended to her daughter that she enroll in a 16-month course in laboratory technician's work given at a nearby university because of her daughter's earlier interest in science and medicine. To Ms. Eaton's great relief, her daughter accepted her advice and has now graduated and is working as a lab technician in a Hartford area hospital. Ruth has recently married a fellow lab technician and the young couple have established themselves in a new apartment in Hartford, which is close to the site of their work.

Ms. Eaton characterized her marriage to Mr. Eaton as an extremely happy and companionable one, in which all decisions were mutually arrived at. Although she herself had come from a family of four children, and her own father had died when she was 4, she never considered that this marriage, which was such a strong one, would be terminated by her husband's death. She spoke at length of her husband's passing as a devastating time in her life. At the same moment that she recognized the honesty of these feelings, she stated that it was impossible to dwell on such feelings. It was an important concern to her to demonstrate to her children, and especially to her son, Samuel, who had expressed terrible feelings of loss and insecurity, that she, as well as his older brother from the first marriage, would look after Samuel and see to his well-being.

There were many examples cited by Ms. Eaton which demonstrated the sense of well-being and solidarity her second family had created. It was customary for her and her husband to take the children on Sunday outings to the zoo or to see the foliage in autumn. She and Mr. Eaton would often stop with the children for dinner out on weekends. They had begun to redo the upstairs apartment. They had made a den for themselves that was off limits to the children. Ms. Eaton proudly showed me the room with a small bar. As she moved about the room one could sense that she moved easily in her mind back to those shared moments and they were a consolation and support to her. Mr. Eaton was able around the house; not only could he do minor repairs, but he was a good craftsman and had paneled their living room with pine. The wood paneling and the leather furniture and wall-to-wall carpeting created an air of warmth and tastefulness in the small, main living room of that apartment.

Their family life-style was altered substantially by Mr. Eaton's death; where before all decisions and disciplining of the children had been shared and they had both assisted the children with their homework, looked after them when they were sick, or cooked when needed, she now assumed responsibility for all aspects of the children's development. Ms. Eaton commented that she often felt like her mother, and it seemed most probable that she derived her strength to go on in part because of the experience of loss of her own father as a child. She had seen her mother make a life for her and her brothers and sister, so that internally she had a prior model and sense of survival through an earlier family ordeal.

Although Ms. Eaton had worked during the early years of her marriage and had had the assistance of a cousin to care for the children, during the years following Mr. Eaton's death the financial circumstances of the family worsened. Ms. Eaton's job as a computer operator and then as a case aide in a federally funded school department program provided an annual salary slightly above the official poverty line. This salary was augmented by veteran's and social security payments for each of the children until they reached the age of 21.

Although the apartment downstairs had been renovated approximately four years previously and could bring in a monthly income of a few hundred dollars, Ms. Eaton had not yet earned that income from the apartment because of her concern for assisting her immediate family members. Prior to her own children living in the apartment and paying modest rental figures, a cousin rented it for minimal rent but also assisted in the care of the children. At considerable cost to her own sense of financial security, Ms. Eaton has supported the needs of her extended family. Indeed, she is looked to, by her brothers and sister, as the main source of strength in their family. Interestingly, when asked to whom she would turn in case of emergencies, she said, "My own children, they have more sense than any of my other relatives."

Ms. Eaton realized after her husband's death that she would need to support both the closeness and the independence as individuals of her children. As they grew up she stressed the need for working together to help and look out for each other. There continued to be a regular time at meals for communication when the children could "let it all hang out." Ms. Eaton instituted a time for herself, when she first came home from work extremely tired. Although at first, she recalled, the children came clamoring around her with news and questions, soon they came to respect her need for repose. Although she had helped them with their homework before her husband's death, this responsibility, along with all the new burdens of their life, seemed too much. She recalled how she had told the children directly, "that's your responsibility now, to work out your homework." She observed that through both of these changes she had made the children less dependent upon her, more self-reliant, and that it was in the children's best interest that she did this. They seemed to accept her new rules.

Ms. Eaton characterized the family as a close one, in which humor and mutual caring and support of each other had carried them through difficult years. One example of their closeness, which demonstrates to this day her children's ability to ask for and receive nurturance from their mother, is their half-humerous, half-serious expectation that she will bring them treats from parties or functions she might attend. Since she and her husband would regularly visit with friends and attend weekend parties, they would regularly bring back treats for the children, and Ms. Eaton, perhaps one could infer, was strengthening this memory of their father at the same moment that she was demonstrating her ability to carry on alone. She said, emphatically, that she never forgot to bring them something.

Ms. Eaton described her own relationship to "causes" and the community in which she lived as basically a nonjoiner of groups or political movements. Although both she and her husband were Protestant, she ceased attending church after her hospitalization nearly two decades ago for the removal of a kidney. She has resided in this same community, in the same house, for 26 years. She is satisfied with the neighborhood, knows her neighbors on either side of her, an Italian and an Armenian family. She stated half in jest, half seriously, "familiarity breeds contempt." She characterized the neighborhood as a mixed working-class community. She felt that police services were relatively unused since the neighborhood was safe and quiet.

Much of Ms. Eaton's leisure time, when she can find some, in the summer and during school holidays, is spent reading and attending good movies. She rarely looks at television unless there is an interesting movie on or programs on different cultures. She regularly reads the paper, and with the resumption of her own schooling this year at Rhode Island State, much of this spare time may be given over to reading or preparing for schoolwork. The family's Sunday routine does not vary much from that during the week. Both she and her son Samuel would have breakfast together and then Samuel would go off to his part-time job. They would have Sunday dinner together; both would read the paper and perhaps watch a few television programs if there was something of interest on. Ms. Eaton stressed that when the children were younger she discouraged them from watching television and urged them to use their imaginations. The children had been active in sports. Her own activities had become more constrained after her husband's death; whereas before she had attended house parties and dances on weekends, she rarely did any of these things as a widow.

When asked to sum up the goals of their family life, Ms. Eaton said she was working towards the independence and security of her children though one didn't ever guarantee such a state. For herself, she would like to grow old gracefully. When we talked about her life moving into a different phase, when all of her children would have completed their schooling or training and were "out in the world," Ms. Eaton recognized the forthcoming lonliness in store for her, but seemed to ward it off by turning to her son nearby and laughingly suggesting that he "stick around for a while." Still, her decision to return to school, which she said she should have begun 10 years ago, is a recognition on her part of the need for her to both improve her financial status and broaden her associations. Certainly her student status will provide her with a possible source of institutional support new in the pattern of her development.

ONE FOR ALL AND ALL FOR ONE
Kathleen Dickinson Rockwood

The Browns' house is well kept but in need of a new coat of paint. The rooms were dimly lit but there seemed to be a great deal of chatter and noise emerging from various rooms. All six children were home, including Mr. and Mrs. Brown and a guest. Jimmy, twenty, was asked to "entertain" me while Mrs. Brown finished up some chores. I could hear her rapidly speaking voice in the background, directing her children to finish the dinner and other tasks. She finally came in, followed by her husband.

The conversation began with questions about their roles as parents within this family; Mrs. Brown did most of the talking, being more gregarious than her husband, a tall, slender, good-looking man of forty-six, who sat back with a pleasant smile on his face most of the time. However, she constantly looked to her husband for recognition and asked for his verbal reassurance. They both came to the consensus that there existed an equal balance of influence between them in the family decision-making, with a few exceptions. Mrs. Brown thought that it was her domain to prepare the meals and see that the children were dressed properly. Her husband controlled the domain of the financial and purchasing aspect of the household. Upon saying that, Mrs. Brown pointed out the sofa, chairs, and other major items which her husband had bought years ago without her help. "He just came home with it all!" But she didn't seem to mind his dominance in this area. She also added with a chuckle, "Honey, you decide on how many children we have, don't you?"

Every so often in the midst of a conversation, Mrs. Brown would correlate what was being said with religion. It became rapidly obvious that politics and other outside forces had little influence on this family. None of the family members was involved in anything within the community, with the exception of the Jehovah's Witnesses. "The family unit is the most important thing to us; everyone in government and politics is so corrupt.

How can they help us achieve a better life in the next world when all their concerns are so worldly? We are not anxious about this life, but are awaiting the times of eternal peace when Armageddon comes." Even though Mrs. Brown expressed these views, it was obvious the beliefs were those of the whole family. Just from observing the family, the close-knit ties became evident, permeating the household with a sense of contentedness. Perhaps much of this could be attributed to their secure allegiance to the Jehovah's Witnesses and their accompanying hopes of future attainment.

Being a Jehovah's Witness calls for living a strict religious life. "If I didn't know that you were morally clean I wouldn't be speaking to you." Because of this and other similar notions the Browns stick to themselves; they restrict their friendships basically to the brothers and sisters of the Kingdom Hall. Mrs. Brown added:

Actually, I feel kind of bad about it, since we've lived here nearly twenty years, but I really don't know any of the neighbors well personally. I know them all by sight and say "hi" but that's it. As a whole the people here are very nice, I just don't have time between my Bible studies, work, and the family. Do you know that I have one neighbor who gives us a turkey every year? That's such a kind thing to do. There's one neighbor who really annoys me though ... the lady next door. She and her sister sit at the windows every day and just put their nose into everyone's business. One day this woman accused my son of stealing something from her car. Well, I found out who did it and told her. Do you think she'd say she was sorry about accusing my son? No, not at all, instead she continually screams at my kids. My children are so good I even can't believe it. I honestly think the neighbors are jealous that they obey me so well. You just can't let your kids go running off into anyone's house. Lord knows there are so many horrible things today with the drug problem and all. I'm scared of that, so I control my children pretty much. The little ones play right outside. If they want to go across the street to ask a friend to come out to play they must ask me first. They do that very thing most of the time. They know that the one thing my husband and I can't tolerate is downright lying and disobeying. They get punished good if that happens. But you see they're good kids, maybe that's because of the way we have brought them up. I've learned that the only way to raise children is to tell them the truth at all times. We tell them everything they might question — from drugs, petting, to other concerns they might have. We don't want our kids learning these things incorrectly on the streets.

Mr. and Mrs. Brown are bringing up their family with values and ideas which both contradict and comply with their parents' past. "First of all," said Mrs. Brown, "I was raised as a Baptist. My mother made us all go to church; she never told us why. Matter of fact, she never answered many of our questions. We don't do that with our kids; we tell them everything. When I was a Baptist we had no hope. Then I took up studying the Bible. We teach our children what the Bible says: this is the right way."

Mrs. Brown confirmed, though, that she really had a nice childhood and family life. Her father was a barber and managed to do pretty well. "My father loved my mother so much he wouldn't let her work. Isn't that nice?" The one thing that really stood out among her many recollections was her education. She said rather proudly that she did excellently in school when she was young. Now, she confided, she didn't feel half as smart as she used to:

When I was in the first grade I was so smart I was promoted to fourth grade. I believe I finished elementary school at 10 years of age. My father made me stay home for a year because he didn't like to see me going through school so fast. I went back to school but my father was still concerned. You see I was just as mature educationally as my grade but didn't act that way. Come senior year my parents took me out of school. Actually, I guess I could have stayed in school but we couldn't even afford food. I was really upset about this and almost had a nervous breakdown. It still bothers me that my parents didn't motivate me to complete school. We lived on a farm, and there were other things for me to do. I used to wonder why my father didn't push me on. When I was younger I thought it was because of lack of love. It's funny, I'm not as smart now, but I still hold the same high hopes. Do you know that I have had the biggest urge to go to the university and be an English teacher? That's what I always wanted to do. But since I can't be a teacher I'm satisfied being a Nurse's Aide. Do you realize I go to work to relax? I have so much to do at home with the kids and all that I actually look forward to going to the hospital. It's such a fulfilling job. You see, people need a little understanding and love; unfortunately they don't get enough.

She went on to speak about Mr. Brown, in reference to his background. "He was brought up as a Baptist too, but he didn't have to go to church as much. His father and mother were real farmers; we just lived on one. They were all very satisfied with what they had, and this is the way that Mr. Brown acts today. He's never been the aggressive type. What I mean is he's always been happy with the same old job; he doesn't like changes. Whereas I could pack up and move tomorrow!" Mr. Brown completed his education only up to the fifth grade level.

Mrs. Brown was very happy to speak about her children. With the exception of the two middle children, the rest are doing about average work in school. She expressed great concern about their educational achievement. Diane, the oldest, is in the twelfth grade and is seventeen years old. She's involved in the Nurse's Aide program in her spare time. In addition, Mrs. Brown commented that she was a tremendous dancer. As far as her future plans go, Diane wants to be a business secretary. Therefore, her mother would be satisfied with her just completing high school. Edward is fifteen and is presently in the tenth grade. In his spare time he plays basketball and goes to the library to read. His greatest interest, though, is to be a mechanic. Mrs. Brown foresees that this might call for mechanic school after high school. She was very worried about the performance of both Cathy, age thirteen, who "thinks she's hot stuff," and James, age eleven; they are barely getting through school. Outside of school Cathy loves to sew or knit, while James spends most of his time catching bugs. Neither of them has expressed interests beyond that. Even though Mrs. Brown didn't want to admit it, Susan, the next to the youngest child, is her most favorite. This little nine-year old is the carbon copy of Mrs. Brown when she was younger. She does well in school and always reads. According to her mother, the child wants to be a teacher, which means a college education. Howard, age six, is the youngest of the family. His most enjoyed pastime is playing outside. He never can have enough of it. He loves trucks and keeps talking about being a truck driver when he grows up. Mrs. Brown stressed that neither she nor her busband were pushing their children towards any specific vocation. There are apparent variations of aspirations within the family. However, she did say: "My children have to go to high school — they can't be dropouts!"

As a family they spend some time together on weekends by

going for rides or going to parks. However, they all have hobbies and have to allocate individual time to put in service. The time when they're all together is dinner and breakfast, with the exception of the father, who has to leave early in the morning. During the night the children are usually at home. At 11:00 p.m. Mrs. Brown goes to work at the hospital while her husband stays home with the family. They both work hard for their children, averaging a sum in combined salaries just below the national median. The house has enough space for the whole family; there's a kitchen, five bedrooms, a living room, dining room, den, and two bathroooms. Mrs. Brown mentioned that they were eventually going to own the house but had to continue monthly payments for approximately five more years. "I don't know if I can wait that long because I want to move back down to South Carolina." Supposedly she and her husband moved to Centerline because of her health, but she's been dying to go back there ever since. The family roots are firmly laid down in this particular neighborhood; therefore, it is doubtful the great move will ever occur.

Mrs. Brown made it a point to show off some of her prize possessions and furniture her husband bought, even if they were many years old. She appeared to be very proud of the household and other possessions. She rattled off all the items they owned: two televisions (one being color), four radios, one record player, and a large, white station wagon.

The problem the two middle children present to their parents is a good example of the concern and care of the Browns, on the one hand, and their lack of understanding of some child-rearing problems, on the other. Mrs. Brown stated that she first thought the two children were so apathetic because they weren't getting enough attention and love. Thus she went out and bought them extra toys and special gifts. This didn't bring about any changes so she and her husband tried talking to the children individually and to their teachers. No real headway has been made to satisfy either parent. At this point the parents are frustrated.

IN SICKNESS AND IN HEALTH
Carol Blanck Tannenhauser and Jill Kirschner Katz

Mrs. Farmer is a middle-aged, attractive, black woman. She was born in a small Pennsylvania town where she lived until her marriage to Mr. Farmer. Mr. Farmer, also a Pennsylvanian by birth, came to Rochester, New York, in search of a job and finally settled upon operating a screw machine for a local factory.

The Farmers live in the suburbs of Rochester. Their neighborhood is primarily a white one, in which only two black families reside. The Farmers have two sons, John, nineteen, and Seth, seventeen ("going on eighteen soon," he insists!). John graduated from high school and is now employed as a messenger at a bank. Seth is presently in his last year in high school.

The Farmers' home is a modest, green ranch house, consisting of six rooms, including three bedrooms. We were particularly impressed with the orderliness of the grounds as we approached the house with a sizeable plot of land and a well-kept rock garden to one side of the entrance. The lawn was carefully trimmed and edged. "That's Seth's job," said Mrs. Farmer. The exterior of the house was bright and cleanly painted with small white shutters brightening the pale green shingles. On the lawn, a group of high school boys, all white except for one later identified as Seth, were tossing a ball between them in a rather lazy game of touch football.

Mr. and Mrs. Farmer had been high school sweethearts, "madly in love since they were sixteen." They had married immediately following Mrs. Farmer's high school graduation, while Mr. Farmer, two years her senior and having completed only ten years of school, was employed at a Pennsylvanian can factory. With the added responsibility of a wife and hearing of industrial job opportunities elsewhere, the couple moved to Rochester, where Mr. Farmer was accepted into a training program to operate a screw machine. Three years later, the Farmers

115

had their first son, John, and moved into their present home. Previously, they had occupied a small two-room apartment. With Mr. Farmer doing well at his job, making employment for Mrs. Farmer unnecessary, Seth was born and the family was doing etremely well both financially and emotionally.

Sixteen years later, "the roof caved in" on the Farmers. Mr. Farmer had been feeling poorly for months, suffering from headaches and sharp pains in his lower back. An examination by the family physician revealed that Mr. Farmer was suffering from a terminal kidney disease that would gradually worsen and intensify, leaving him bedridden and unable to work. What was worse, the disease was revealed to be genetically transmitted, and the early signs were detected in the then nine-year-old John. As the year progressed, the disease weakened Mr. Farmer, causing him first to leave his job, and confining him to his bed, and finally making it necessary for him to be admitted to the hospital. The Farmer family, previously so secure and promising, faced a crisis in its stability, placing most of the burden for survival upon Mrs. Farmer.

Determined to instill in her young sons a sense of security and well-being, she found a job as a maid in a university fraternity house, and worked evenings in a supermarket. Convinced that a strong parent's presence was imperative to their emotional stability, she managed to confine her working hours to the times at which they were in school, or involved with their homework and was always home by 8:00 p.m., so that the three of them could go together to the hospital to visit their father. This routine kept up until John was old enough and able to get a job washing windows after school, thus allowing Mrs. Farmer to give up her own evening job.

So the Farmers held together, despite the unfortunate odds of a sick father unable to leave the hospital. Mrs. Farmer's income added to the payment of medical bills; however, the majority of them were handled by compensation and state funds. The family, according to Mrs. Farmer, became closer as a result of Mr. Farmer's illness and began eating meals together whereas they previously had "just grabbed whatever was around." "I guess we sort of had a combined guilty conscience — what with

Hal so sick," commented Mrs. Farmer. The family developed a closeness and consideration for each other, learning to substitute family decisions and responsibility for the previous authority of the now absent Mr. Farmer.

The Farmer boys did average work in high school and proceeded with the knowledge that "no matter what, they would finish." When Seth was old enough, he too got a job with the janitorial company where John was employed, and thus, the family income was again supplemented. Mrs. Farmer became the cook for the fraternity at which she was previously a maid, again raising their income and adding security to their existence.

Presently the Farmer family appears stable, close, and promising. Mrs. Farmer enjoys cooking for the fraternity brothers, and loves the closeness she has developed with them. Her weekday routine, followed six days out of seven, consists of rising at 6:30 a.m. to cook breakfast for her sons, shopping, and heading to the university in time to prepare lunch for forty hungry brothers. She works until 6:00 p.m. and is home by 6:15 p.m. in time to prepare and serve dinner to her own sons at 7:00, which is the family's regular dinnertime. The three eat together and then Mrs. Farmer does the dishes while John and Seth retire to their "makeshift basketball court to shoot the hoops," for about a half hour following dinner. Then at 8:00, Seth pulls the family's old car from the garage and the family heads for the hospital to spend an hour with their father. They each spend fifteen minutes alone with Mr. Farmer relating personal needs and events, and then conclude the visit with the four of them together, concentrating on cheering up and encouraging Mr. Farmer. They are home by 9:00 p.m., at which time John heads for his girlfriend's house and Seth to his homework, leaving a tired Mrs. Farmer to collapse in her "favorite" soft chair in front of a TV.

Out of necessity Mrs. Farmer has become the everyday head of the family. However, Mr. Farmer is still consulted on important decisions and plans. Even when Mr. Farmer was still living at home, Mrs. Farmer took an active part in raising the children. Having completed more education than her husband, she always helped the boys with their homework and in addition, took care of them when they were ill, decided what to serve for meals, cooked, helped them decide upon their clothing, went to school to talk with their teachers, decided upon the house they would live in, helped the boys find part-time work against Mr. Farmer's wishes, and decided upon what furniture to buy — "since I have to clean it," she joked. Mr. Farmer always handled the financial aspects of the family such as the children's allowances and what the family could afford to spend money on. Other important decisions were made as a group in an open-minded and fair manner.

"With their father gone I try especially hard to be open-minded with the boys. They even know what bills are coming in and how and when I pay them. If I refuse them something, you can be sure they know why. I encourage their independence and disagreement because I have to with Hal gone. But I'm not one of these old people who can't be wrong — I do apologize to them."

Even discipline is discussed in the Farmer household, with the offender present. "But my boys don't need much — they feel a responsibility to behave because of Hal's condition, I guess — neither of them has ever been in any serious trouble either at school or with the police."

As far as ideals and goals for her children, Mrs. Farmer leaves the final decision to her sons. She is a Protestant by birth and has seen to the baptism of her sons. However, they are aware that they are free to choose their own religion if they desire to change. This policy carries through to their employment futures as well. "John is a steady, family man — he has always been — I wish him only a wife whom he loves and who can give him children. Seth has always wanted to be a baseball player — I hope he makes it." Mrs. Farmer holds no stock in the idea that everyone should go on to college. According to her, John was never a student, so she insisted only that he finish high school. Seth is different, he wishes to go on to college, so his desire becomes a family decision, for college for Seth would mean sacrifices by everyone. Therefore, everyone has a say in the ultimate decision. As far as Mrs. Farmer is concerned , her goals for her sons are that they grow into "good, healthy, honest, clean men," and anything more is asking too much.

Mrs. Farmer is an energetic woman completely satisfied and involved in the affairs of her neighborhood. The area is classified as a white, working-class one, "filled with children who are well-behaved to the point that we never see the police at all!" Most of the couples belong to both the Church clubs, and a neighborhood service organization. The latter runs charity drives and picnics. In addition, Mrs. Farmer is active in the PTA and attends all the school athletic events in which her son Seth participates.

As far as social action and civil rights, Mrs. Farmer remains passive. In fact, she considers herself an "outcast" from the current black freedom movement as a result of her location in a white neighborhood. She describes herself and for the most part her sons, as "not politically-minded at all," and seemed to have no commitment whatsoever to black protest. Her attitude seems to suggest that she has enough trouble keeping her own family going. She is a hard-working sincere woman, co-existing happily with her neighbors. She called hers a safe neighborhood, filled with people she knows (20-30), "who aren't rich and who don't live on top of each other, without racial prejudice, where you can always count on people, but where everyone minds their own business 'cause they're busy trying to make a living." Her only complaint was the absence of sidewalks and bus lines which cause minor inconvenience but no real problem. As far as Mrs. Farmer was concerned, she "wouldn't move even if she could afford to."

John, age nineteen, the older of the Farmer sons, is a serious-minded boy, perhaps as a result of his father's illness, or perhaps because of his own condition. He was never an outstanding student, but was always well liked by his peers and active in high school sports. However, in his junior year his own kidney condition worsened and he was forced to resign from the football team of which he was once captain. He was never a college-oriented student and always intended to only finish high school; that he did with a blaze of glory, for in his senior year he was presented the "Most Well Liked Senior Award" by the town civic association.

After high school John, who continues to live at home, secured a position at a bank where he now works as a messenger with a chance of promotion after one year's employment. In addition, he attends night school financed by the bank, but views it with extreme distaste. "I never was one for school," he smiled apologetically. But John is happy, except when he thinks of his father. He has a "great job, and an out-of-sight girl" he hopes to marry some day and with whom he hopes to raise a family. In the meantime, he loves his family and contributes heavily to their sustenance — "It's the least I can do for Mom!"

Seth, age seventeen, a senior in high school, loves being a student and is intricately involved in the athletic program. He spends his days in classes and his afternoons working out with the different teams of which he is a vital part. He plays basketball, baseball, and was named an all-state wrestling champion last winter. Seth is a personable, bright youth, seemingly endowed with his mother's sense of humor. At school he is a part of a high school fraternity, and in addition works from 4:30 to 7:00 p.m. for a janitorial firm, washing windows. This is Seth's contribution to the financial state of his family.

Seth plans to go on to college with the hope of becoming either a professional baseball player, or a recreational director. He recently received an offer from a major league baseball organization to go on to school, financed by it, and then enter into a training program perhaps someday to play major league ball. As of now his future is uncertain, but his athletic prowess seems to indicate that he will probably receive financial aid and thus be able to attain a college education.

Sundays are a day for togetherness at the Farmer home. Mrs. Farmer rises at 7:00 a.m. and "after two cups of coffee and six cigarettes!" manages to get going. The family eats breakfast together and then drives to church for the 10:00 a.m. mass. They're home by noon, at which time Mrs. Farmer prepares lunch. After that, "the records go on — the TV is blaring — John and his girl listen to music and Seth is shushing everyone because one game or another is on!" Mrs. Farmer gathers the wash and does the week's laundry. Then she gives the dog a bath, cleans the house and is back to the kitchen to cook again!

After dinner it's ironing time and the nightly routine begins. "I cook — they eat — I clean — they mess up. John gets on the phone — Seth does his homework — Seth yells at John to get off the phone, John gets off the phone — Seth gets on the phone — I yell at Seth to get off the phone — and we go to bed."

The Farmers, despite Mr. Farmer's progressive disease, are stable. Mrs. Farmer is a hard-working, sensible, and loving mother and these qualities are reflected in her sons, who are diligent, intelligent young men. Mrs. Farmer seems to have injected a sense of stability in the boys, and both look forward to the day that they will have their own families. Both agree upon one point regarding their future families and that is, "my wife won't have to work like Mom!" The boys have a strong sense of financial conditions and through their mother's guidance have learned to expect only what is within their grasp, or else to go out and work for anything more they desire. As Seth puts it, "Decisions for us are not taken for granted like they are with the other kids around here. I can't just naturally go on to school, 'cause my mother doesn't have three or four thousand dollars to throw around — and I have to really want it and then we all have to work for it."

Mrs. Farmer is nearing the end of her term as a full-time mother, for her sons are rapidly approaching manhood, soon to have other homes and families of their own. John is deeply in love with a seventeen-year old girl, but feels that they must wait until he is established before getting married. Again, the sence of responsibility of the mother has been passed on to the son. Seth, when asked if he was considering marriage at all, simply laughed.

SEVEN CHILDREN STRONG
Daniel G. Lowengard

I arrived at Mr. Wilson's house at 6:50 p.m. Unfortunately it was dark and I couldn't see much of his house or property. The Wilsons own the dirt road leading to their house. The area was mostly rocks and junk with a few trees: but with the potential to be very beautiful. "Someday, I'll get a chance to clean the place up," Mr. Wilson told me. There was a little stream on the property which separated the house and the dirt road, a foot-thick slab of concrete provided a bridge. The house was obviously isolated, but other houses were in sight and walking distance.

The Wilson living room is small but cozy; it had a broken couch, two wooden chairs, and an old piano. The kitchen is bigger than the living room. A few of the cupboards were broken but it was in much better shape than the rest of the house. Mr. Wilson had redone the whole kitchen himself a few years ago.

Mrs. Wilson is tall and attractive but her face showed the years of work and she looked easily her thirty-six years. Mrs. Wilson didn't sit in the kitchen, but rather chose the adjoining living room. She didn't say much except to supply dates and ages, which her husband usually didn't know.

Mr. Wilson is tall and muscular, had sideburns which met his mustache. He, like his wife, had the rugged look and his thirty-seven years were equally apparent. His hands told the story; they were huge and heavily calloused. His right thumb was abnormally large from an accident in a woodshop where it was smashed. Nevertheless, his life revolved around the use of his hands. We started the interview with talk of his family.

Mr. and Mrs. Wilson have seven children from the ages of nine to nineteen, all living at home. The first five were born in the South: Cynthia, nineteen; Charles, eighteen; Nelson, seventeen; Leda, fourteen; and Norton, twelve. They were born in

Georgia. Eleven years ago the Wilsons moved north to York, Pennsylvania. In York they lived with three other families: Mr. Wilson's parents, Mr. Wilson's sister's family, and his brother's family. Andrea, ten, and Alex, nine, joined the family; then the house was severely overcrowded — four to six in a room. The contrast between the Wilsons' old home and new one is immense. Now, they have almost an abundance of room. The family is exceptionally pleased with the change. This change has had an effect on their interaction, or lack of, with the community, but this will be discussed later.

Cynthia's child (six months old, whose father is white and did not marry Cynthia), has provided "no real added burden" Mr. Wilson said. "Everyone realizes they must do a little more and they do." He thinks it has brought the family a little closer together. He explained that Mrs. Wilson was pregnant at about the same time, so the experience did not shatter him or his wife as it might have in a different setting.

Cynthia's life has changed more than the family's from this experience. She was forced to leave the State College to go to the local Community College in order to raise her child. Mr. Wilson said she does not resent the child, but she does resent the father of the child. Her hatred for whites is an outgrowth of this. Mr. Wilson said, "fortunately the other children have not adopted similar views." He is glad that Cynthia did stay in school. "Nowadays you can't do anything without an education."

Mr. and Mrs. Wilson quit school in the eleventh grade to get married; both went to work immediately to raise a family. Mr. Wilson realizes the difficulty in earning enough to raise a family, if one's education is inadequate. He is trying to encourage Charles to "get going;" Charles is the only one having any trouble in school and it is only minimal. Nelson is in an accelerated program and will go to college next year. Leda, Norton, Andrea, and Alex are all in public school doing "average or better work," said a proud father.

We discussed in detail the differences in Northern and Southern schools. He preferred the South because, as he described it, "There, you got an education. You came out of high school with a trade and knowin' what you wanted to do. In the North you graduate and you are still lost." Time and time again he would emphasize college as "a must."

In the Wilson household everyone who can work does just that. Mr. Wilson works over sixty-two hours per week. When he came North he was qualified to be a barber, but without money to start his own business, and due to discrimination in barber unions, he had to look for something else. For the past eleven years he has been the janitor at a temple in York. At night he does similar work for many "important people" in York. He took great pride in his associations with these people and the members of the temple. Mr. Wilson says he know every member of the temple and can even say how many kids each member has and what they are doing. This is quite a feat considering the temple is the largest temple in the city for Conservative Jews. Mr. Wilson considers himself "close to the Jewish people." If Mr. Wilson has any left-over time he spends it fixing the house, though he admits there is little time for that. He has hopes of setting up a wood shop in the garage and pursuing that work while dropping the other extra jobs.

Mrs. Wilson is a Nurse's Aide at the municipal hospital and has been working there since they moved north. She has never been able to take time from work to raise the kids. None of the children has ever been trouble with the police, and all but one are doing well in school. Mr. Wilson does wish that his wife did not have to work but realizes at the present time that it is impossible.

Charles works for the *News,* where he runs errands and does odd jobs. Nelson works at a chain restaurant; both put in fifteen to twenty hours per week. Norton is a paper boy for the *News*, and Alex helps, of course. If there is a basic theme to this family it is helping each other. Everyone realizes that financially they aren't well off, so everyone pitches in (Norton shares his money with the little ones). Everyone knows the baby must be taken care of, so they all help Cynthia. These seemingly adverse conditions are transposed into a unifying force.

Mr. Wilson was very proud that he and his family make do on what they make. The combined family income is less than the national median but above the poverty line. Out of their limited funds the family meets household expenses and pays money on the mortgage. Mrs. Wilson contributes a little less than half of the total income. The Wilsons are not on welfare, and they are quite proud that they are not — "that's why I work sixty-five hours a week."

Although Baptists, the Wilsons rarely attend church. Mr. Wilson said, "religion is not that important. The church does not do anything for people, expecially black people." Mr. Wilson went on to say that black people don't have enough time for the church. For him Sunday is the only day he can rest. Furthermore, the church speaks of things that aren't close to the reality of his everyday life.

He sends Leda, Andrea, and Alex to church because he feels "it's good for the young ones to hear about God somewhere besides in the home." Charles, Nelson, and Norton all work on Sunday, so they can "get out of it."

Although the Wilson family has a modest income, the mother works, and the family is large, this family should be classified as stable. One possible explanation is the tendency for the "tough to get going, when the going gets tough."

Mr. Wilson said there is little reason for strict discipline in his home because the kids are all "pretty good, and have been taught to work things out among themselves." If there is reason for discipline, both parents do it, and it is usually in the form of a "talk" which is "better than a spanking." He wants his children to be independent, though he thinks it is the parents' responsibility to know where the children are at night.

The Wilson family has three groups. Cynthia is usually the loner, and solves problems herself or else goes to her mother. Charles and Nelson form a second group, and can usually work things out themselves, though Mr. Wilson helps. The final group of Leda, Norton, Andrea, and Alex tend to get into more "trouble" than the others. But as Mr. Wilson explains, "kids are kids and you can't expect them to be perfect." Norton is pretty much the leader of this last group; he "likes meeting people, and is by far the most outgoing one in the family."

Things like homework, spending money, and clothing are

pretty much left up to the individual. Mr. and Mrs. Wilson will help with such decisions but they like to see the kids "do it on their own." There is, however, a clear indication that the boys seek out their father for help, whereas the girls go to their mother.

BLEST BE THE CHILD THAT BINDS
Nancy Martin

The "man of the house" was very pleasant and friendly, and it was with him that this interview was conducted. Mr. Harold Henderson is the head of a small, black family of three — husband, wife, and three-year-old daughter. The family resides in a publicly assisted housing development in Boston, Massachusetts.

Mr. Henderson, born in Texas 55 years ago, grew up in a family that consisted of his mother and three other children. Apparently his father left home soon after he was born because Mr. Henderson has no recollection of him at all. He said that his mother had taken good care of them; they never starved, but were quite poor. Mr. Henderson attended public school and completed the tenth grade. Then he dropped out because he needed money and felt that he should not depend on this mother any longer. He spoke quite highly of her, and said that she taught him all "the good things" he knows. His brothers and sisters he sees only occasionally because they are scattered widely through the states; and one sister lives in another country.

When he was twenty-three he decided to migrate North. He came to Boston. There, he got married; a son, Jesse, was born. He is an adult and now lives in Los Angeles.

At age thirty-two, Mr. Henderson began working for a large company in Boston, as a custodian, where he is still employed.

Mr. Henderson's first wife died. He lived as a widower for several years. Five years ago, he married again and now has a second child, a three-year-old daughter.

Before moving into the housing development, Mr. and Mrs. Henderson lived in a smaller apartment on the south side of the city. It was an old apartment, difficult to keep clean, he said. Mr. and Mrs. Henderson are satisfied with their present home of almost one year. It is new, clean, and they feel has wonderful facilities for what they are paying. There is a garbage disposal in the kitchen, which Mrs. Henderson "just loves," a parking area below the apartments, laundry facilities in each building, and a play area for children. Mr. Henderson said that they would stay in this housing development indefinitely, if they were permitted to do so. The apartment has two bedrooms, a kitchen, living and dining area, bathroom, and storage closet — much more than they ever had, and for a better price too. They were well pleased with their new housing.

Aside from his regular job, Mr. Henderson also worked as custodian and rent collector for his landlord before moving into the development. He really disliked that because, he said, it made him "the bad man" of the area. He was the one who had to make reports, receive the complaints on behalf of the landlord, and collect the rent. Few people in his old apartment building were fond of him. Also, the Henderson family describ-ed the area surrounding his former dwelling as crowded and dangerous. Thus, they were happy to move.

Mr. Henderson has been working in his present job for seventeen years. He likes the work and said that he is going to stay with this company until he retires. He know the people well with whom he works. Moreover, he believes that staying with the same company is good security for him. He is a custodian and also does some pick-up and delivery work when he is asked to. A steady worker, Mr. Henderson hasn't missed a day from work in five years. He is extremely proud of this record.

Mrs. Henderson doesn't work outside the home. He feels that she is a good wife and mother, and that he has been a good husband and father. He says that he has tried his best to provide well for his family, and feels that he has been quite successful. He has arranged so that every week, a certain amount of his check is taken out by a credit union, and held for his rent and future savings. This practice is followed, Mr. Henderson said, because he learned the hard way that it was difficult to get home Friday afternoons with a whole check. It is much safer for the credit union to deduct the rent and savings from his pay before he gets it.

Mr. Henderson is very active in the church, which is the

center of most of his activities. He is an usher and never misses a Sunday unless it cannot be avoided. He goes on trips with church groups and participates in most of the church social functions. His wife goes with him at times, but not as often as he would like her to. Mr. Henderson also said that he is a member of the Masons.

Mr. Henderson admitted that he loves parties and really enjoys drinking, but usually confines his "boozing" to the nights out with the boys because his wife feels differently about it.

Cooking is one among several things in the home Mr. Henderson likes to do. When he was younger, he worked as a short-order cook. Now he doesn't have much opportunity to cook.

Mr. Henderson is very proud of and loves his daughter a great deal. He said that whenever he is not with her (if he goes on a trip, or his wife and daughter go away) he misses her very much. He said that he and his wife hope that their daughter will finish school and become either a school teacher or a secretary, which they feel are respectable and worthwhile positions for a woman.

The family's weekdays are fairly consistent. Mr. Henderson wakes up first, eats breakfast alone, and leaves for work. He is gone all day from 7:30 a.m. until about 5:00 p.m. Mrs. Henderson and their daughter get up after he leaves and have their breakfast. Mrs. Henderson does her housework, may go to visit some friends in the morning or have visitors in for coffee while Betty, their daughter, amuses herself or plays with the children of her mother's friends. The Hendersons have only one car which Mr. Henderson must drive to work; so Mrs. Henderson tends to visit neighbors in the area who are within walking distance.

At lunch time Mrs. Henderson and Betty eat together, and since Mr. Henderson is at work, he eats with his friends. After lunch Betty takes a short nap, during which time her mother either relaxes, watching television, or does some laundry or general housework. Later in the afternoon, if she needs groceries, she and her daughter, and sometimes some friends, walk to the store and shop.

Mr. Henderson comes home about 5:00 p.m. and the family has dinner at about 5:30. He said that he always comes home right after work. If he is planning to go out, then he leaves from home, but never goes elsewhere directly from work. At night, after dinner, Mr. Henderson plays with their daughter while Mrs. Henderson cleans up. In the evening he reads the paper and watches television unless he has a church meeting or some other activity to go to. He usually heads for bed around midnight — sometimes Mrs. Henderson goes earlier, or later, depending on what she is doing.

On weekends, a Sunday for instance, Mr. and Mrs. Henderson get up about 8:00 a.m. Mr. Henderson notes that rising time depends somewhat on what he has done the night before. The family has breakfast, usually together, then he leaves for church at 10:50 a.m. Sometimes they all go together but most often he goes alone. (Mr. Henderson really enjoys church and stays there usually until about 2:00 p.m. Mr. Henderson is well-known, liked, and respected at his church). In the afternoon he reads the paper, plays with Betty. The family eats dinner at 4:00 p.m. Sometimes they all go for a walk or drive, and sometimes they stay at home. Time for them on Sunday is not structured — they do what they feel like doing, sometimes individually, sometimes together.

Mr. Henderson is young-looking and acting, for his age, and says strongly, "I really love living." One might classify him a conservative and a very practical person in the matters that involve his family and finances. He has learned from his mistakes and looks at them as good teaching experiences. He is warm and friendly.

Mrs. Henderson appears to be a completely different type of person, compared with her husband. She is younger than he, but does not seem to possess the energy, and ambition that he exhibits. She has a quiet and suspecting manner. She has a few activities outside the home, but does not enjoy the same activities that her husband enjoys.

The one and important sharing that this couple experiences is their daughter. Betty is the target of Mr. Henderson's love. She is a happy child and relates well to her father and mother.

At times Mr. Henderson seems rather lonely, and somewhat dissatisfied with his marriage. He loves being involved in activities and with other people, but his wife does not seem to share his interests. Outside the home, they do little together. Mr. Henderson's love for their daughter seems to be the tie that binds him to his wife and their home.

The family structure seems to be equalitarian in a general sense. Mrs. Henderson takes care of most things within the home. Mr. Henderson takes care of matters outside the home. They both share in the responsibility of caring for their daughter.

7 POOR REBELS

All six of the poor black families are city dwellers who live in apartments in the inner city. Four of the six households are single-parent and two consist of husband and wife. The four single-parent households are headed by mothers. In two of these households, a boyfriend visits often and relates to the children as a father would. Three of the single-parent households are that way because of divorce; the fourth single parent never married. Only two of the households had adult parents who were gainfully employed. In all other households, including the two two-parent units, the fathers and mothers were unemployed; however, the family received some income in one two-parent home by taking in foster children.

Education for all was limited. Only one parent was a high school graduate. All other parents in these households were either high school dropouts — the experience of three mothers and one father — or received less than a grade school education.

The Helen Jones family is a one-child family in which the mother is unemployed and receives public welfare; she had never married. The Simmons household consists of four offspring and one grandchild, although only three offspring and a grandchild live at home. The mother is unemployed, divorced, and receives welfare. The Harris home is the residence for two children and a divorced mother who works with a federally funded community development program. The Fishers, a two-parent kinship unit, have eight children, who have all grown up and left home. The father worked in a bakery but recently lost his job and cannot find work; he and his wife take in foster children for pay and babysit their grandchildren. The other Jones family is headed by Coreen Jones. It is a single-parent household because of divorce and consists of the mother, who is a cleaning woman, four children, and a grandmother. The Butler family consists of husband and wife and one child. The husband was a stockroom attendant but is out of work. This is a second marriage; the two decided that the mother should be a homemaker.

DOWN BUT NOT OUT
Kristen Haggman Mitchell

Helen Jones cannot decipher her mother's first name on her birth certificate or adoption papers; it is either Helene or Thelma, and of her she has neither recollection nor information. Helen Jones was born in Cleveland 27 years ago. Sometime during the first two years of her life, she moved from Chicago to Philadelphia and was placed for adoption when she was 2 years old. She was adopted by a childless black couple. She can remember only fragments of the first eight years of her life, such as the names of the various streets on which she lived. Her most vivid memory was spending days with her father ("me and him alone"). Also, she remembers getting measles and staying home when she was in the second grade; about that time, her cousin came to live with the family when her child was born. Helen attended first, second, and third grades in an inner-city public school and was enrolled in a private church-sponsored school for the fourth grade.

Helen feels that her life changed dramatically at that time. She attributes this to a particular incident that she recalls with indignation. One afternoon, her mother picked her up from school and as they walked home, her mother said to her, "Don't tell anyone you're adopted." Two days later, her mother handed Helen a book about adoption. Helen said that she never understood the meaning of adoption before and that her mother never sat down and explained anything. "Boom! that was that. I felt like I belonged to no one and no where."

Helen Jones went on a stealing binge; she took books, staples, notebooks, and pencils from local stores and school. She says that she would walk into a store and walk out with as much as she could hide. She began to lie about her activities to her mother, who apparently had become suspicious about the new items appearing in the house. For the next two years, Helen continued to lie and steal. When her mother eventually dis-

134

covered that Helen was stealing, she beat her over the head with a hairbrush. Helen says that she eventually stopped stealing because her mother "just beat it out of me." She said that her father never touched her. Meanwhile, she stole pencils, notebooks, and paper at the private school and was caught. The priest at the school "tried to find out why, but it didn't help much." Helen says that she couldn't tell him why she had stolen the things because she "honestly didn't know." His response and solution was to ask her to get down on her knees with him and pray. Helen said that she did so because she was "willing to please anyone to get them to shut up and get off my back."

The next year, Helen returned to the public school presumably because her parents couldn't afford the private school. This was the explanation given but Helen doubts it; she feels that she was thrown out. In the fifth grade, her teacher told her that she was a "brilliant child and had to slow down with the other kids in the class." Helen describes this experience as "the beginning of my downfall; a lot of creativity was destroyed in me." The following year, at the age of eleven, she was sent to boarding school. She remembers writing letters home telling her parents how much she hated the place. Her parents then moved to a suburban community in the same metropolitan area; she returned home and enrolled in a local suburban public school.

Concerning her suburban school experience, she says, "Do you know what it's like to be in a crowded room and feel lonely?" Her mother, whom Helen calls "a middle-class, materialistic snob," "inspected" her friends "like a piece of meat." Everyone Helen brought home had to be "examined" by her mother. Helen felt that her father never intervened on her behalf. Life became unbearable between mother and daughter. Helen's mother began to drink heavily. At the age of 14, precipitated by an argument with her inebriated mother, Helen ran away. She stayed away from home for ten days and lived in Philadelphia in a commune crash-pad. Helen returned home but ran away again, a year later, because of mother's "drinking, fantastic restrictions, and noncompromising attitude." She stayed away longer this time, but returned. She and her mother had "nightly rows." It was during one of these rows that her father had a heart attack. Shortly thereafter, at the age of 16, she ran away from home a third time.

She took the bus to Boston and "hung out" with the street people. She met a young man and together they hitched around the country. They ended up in California; there they ended their relationship. Soon afterward, Helen was "busted" for vagrancy and loitering and was sent to a detention center. After a week there, she was flown home to Philadelphia and was placed in a detention facility for a month. In detention she said she "flipped, freaked, and got hysterical; people flew away from me in all directions and I threw around chairs and smashed windows. The matron stopped me, after a lot of struggling, at the point when I was about to smash my hand into some grating." Helen said that she was "tense and nervous" afterwards and was transferred to a state-run school for girls. She stayed there for nine months and "freaked out" again and told a nun "where she could go and where she could stick it." On her seventeenth birthday, just a few months short of her scheduled return home, she told her mother that unless she got her out of there, she would run. Helen and her mother went into court and made a "deal" with the judge whereby Helen could go to summer school and return to high school as a senior in the fall. For the entire summer, Helen says that she was a "good girl." For the first time, Helen felt that "it looked like things were going to work out."

Helen returned to the suburban public high school that fall. For a reason she can't understand and does not know, she went on a "sleeping binge." She would get up in the morning, go to school, come home, and go immediately to sleep. Three days later, her parents called a doctor who, according to her report, told Helen's parents to wake her up and not let her sleep. When her parents tried to awaken her, she "flipped out again. There was no calming me down." The parents, "not knowing what to do," called the police, who took Helen to the hospital. She reports that the police then returned her to her home, reassured her that was all right to sleep, and told her parents to let her alone.

By November of her senior year, Helen was cutting school

and fighting constantly with her mother. In December, she ran away from home and stayed on the streets. From January until the following summer, Helen hitch-hiked across the country alone, spending a few months "here and there." She returned home for two weeks, and then left. That summer she began to deal in "junk" and "hustle." She met Tim, "the most unreliable man she has ever met." The following December, she decided to "kick" heroin. She stayed with Tim while she was "kicking the habit." She remembers having intercourse with Tim once. When the winter came, she left Philadelphia and hitched again across the country alone. It was the best hitching expedition she had ever had, she said. People took her into their homes readily. She recalls having Christmas dinner with a family in Illinois who took her a week later to Arizona. It was there that she discovered that she was pregnant. Helen called her mother, who insisted that she come home.

When Helen returned home, her mother "tried to talk her into an abortion." Helen "thought and thought about it" until one day, she woke up and decided that she was going to keep the baby. Her mother told her that "she wasn't going to have a grown woman in the house with a kid without a man." She kicked Helen out.

Helen Jones lived in rooming houses and went on welfare for the next few months. She knew many people on the streets, but had no one with whom she was intimately involved and who could support her in a minimal way. After her baby was born, there was a time lag between receipt of general relief and aid for dependent children. Helen did not get the increased allotment for several months. She "hustled" to earn money for "formula, diapers, and rent." For one month, October, she placed her son in a foster home in order to "get her shit together," as she put it. She took him back, stayed another month in the rooming house, and returned home ("my mother took me back"). Three-quarters of her welfare check was demanded by her mother "for rent." Around Christmas time, Helen Jones was talking to her friend on the telephone. They were discussing their New Year's Eve plans and Helen says she was apparently "daydreaming." Her mother came into the room and accused Helen of looking like she was on "junk" again. She attacked Helen with a pair of scissors. For the next two weeks the tension was so bad that Helen couldn't stay in the same room with her mother.

In January, Helen's mother was admitted into the hospital for internal blockage. For two weeks Helen did not visit her mother. One day Helen received a call from the hospital. She found her father, who had gone out for breakfast. They rushed to the hospital and were told her mother had died of a blood clot in the lung. The entire family blamed her, Helen said, for not visiting her mother while she was hospitalized. In March, Helen moved away from home and found an apartment, in which she is presently living with her son. She started taking courses at Temple University. Finding school, "on top of everything else," more than she could handle, she flunked out. Her central goal, she says, is to return to school and to get off welfare.

RESIDENCE AND COMMUNITY

Helen Jones and her child live in a rented flat with a kitchen, bedroom, living room, and bathroom. She has a radio, television, and telephone but no clock. Her income is minimal and is supplemented by food stamps. She describes the neighborhood as black working class. She doesn't like where she lives because, although the area has a reputation for being "safe," the street lighting at night is poor and she fears robbery. To avoid this, she always takes her child with her wherever she goes after dark because she feels that "no one would bother a mother with a child." Generally, "things are quiet," and there is "no trouble." She thinks that she is getting a "good deal" on her apartment rent. She knows about five other people who live near her, but not well enough to ask for assistance. She doesn't feel that she is in a "community, because in a community, people speak to one another on the streets and the children play together." When she needs help, she turns to her father, her aunt, and her cousin, in that order.

DAILY ACTIVITIES

On the day preceding the day of this interview, which was typical in her life, Helen got up at 8:30 a.m., fixed breakfast for her child and for herself, bathed, and got dressed. She had a ten o'clock doctor's appointment and was out of the house by 9:30. She tells time by the radio and the telephone time service. For appointments, she allows forty-five minutes to an hour from the time she leaves home and arrives at the appointed place. She is always punctual. She and her child stayed at the doctor's office for about an hour and arrived home around noontime. ("The kids had gone in from the playground.") She and her child "hung outside in front of the house and went in around 2:00." Helen then fixed lunch. For the rest of the afternoon, her child ran around the house and Helen read. She cooked dinner earlier than usual (at 6:00 p.m.), read until 8:00, put her child to bed, and cleaned up three rooms. She watched television and went to bed at 11:30. Helen recalled the events of the day easily, although she says that she is usually not aware of how the days pass. On other typical days there is food shopping, appointments (doctor, welfare), more television watching, and housekeeping duties (cleaning and laundry). On some nights, she goes out with a friend to "clubs" and socializes in the bars or after-hour places.

DECISION-MAKING AND PLANNING MODES

When Helen Jones has a particular problem which demands a decision, she will sit down and think about it for a while. Then she will ignore it. She says that it takes a while for her to make up her mind, that she has to feel "really sure and secure." Oftentimes, she will go around in "circles, examining the pros and cons, leave it alone, go back to it, and then it comes to her." Concerning her child, she says that "being a parent requires security," and that she is aware of her control over her son's life. For that reason, she really has to "feel good about whatever it is." Her most recent big decision concerns the possibility of sending her son down South with his aunt for the summer. Such as arrangement, she felt, would allow her to organize her life, make specific plans to return to school and to put her child into daycare, and generally give herself "breathing space." She feels that this took serious thought, particularly because she says that she feels terrible when her child goes away even for a night. She talked to her aunt and cousin about it all and received reassurance from them that summer care of her son wouldn't be "too much of a burden." Generally, Helen feels good about the decisions that she has made in the past, although she says that sometimes she gets into them and finds that she's gone over her head. She cites returning to school two years ago as an example of this.

As far as future planning is concerned, Helen does not look far ahead. She says that she can plan in "terms of a year, but gets frustrated by that." She feels that "it is hard to say that you want to do something, because something will come along and destroy it. ... You just don't know what's going to catch you. I can say that I want to and try it and go ahead and make the effort, but ..." She can't "picture" herself in five years. She thinks that she is "the kind of person who dies young," by forty, and that it's hard enough for her to plan for the month. She deals with her child as he grows "day by day," and thinks that it will be easier to plan ahead "once he gets into school." Being a single parent, she believes, one has "to plan and be sure and feel secure." She doesn't feel secure and thinks that she has "a lot to deal with," so she does things "day by day."

IDEALS AND CHILD

Helen Jones states that her son "surprises" her all the time. He has an "outgoing personality," an extroverted style, and "says 'hi' to everyone." She thinks that he has a "really good personality." She wants to "let him go as he is doing." Concerning morals, Helen says, "Everyone has an attitude about right and wrong and that is hard to say, you know, what to do sometimes. All I can do for my son is to try to be as understanding as possible ... to sit down and listen to what he has to say. I don't want to make the same mistakes. In my family, there was not much listening." She feels that she is opening good lines of communication that will "really stay together," that he is learning right from wrong now, "by knowing what he can get into and can't." Helen emphatically feels one thing: she is grateful that "he's not spoiled."

DISCIPLINE AND CHILD

Helen Jones feels that she has a problem being a single parent. She can become easily frustrated and angry and believes that her child can very easily "become the victim" of her frustration. She claims, nevertheless, that she rarely spanks him and that "discipline is not a heavy thing" in her house. He son, she thinks, "has a lot of freedom to a point," and that they have a good understanding of what he can or cannot do. Under "extreme circumstances" — such as danger — and/or after she has told him three times, she will spank him. Thereafter, he usually won't do it again and, ordinarily, she never has to tell him anything more than once. Also, Helen has definite ideas about anger. She thinks that "if you hold it inside you, it can destroy you." She, therefore, encourages her son to "get angry." He usually gets mad when his mother tells him not to do something. She responds by telling him "to go ahead and be angry, but what I'm telling you is law."

CHILD AND EDUCATION

Helen Jones wants her son "to have a quality education," which means to her "having people, teachers, look at him beyond his race." ("They classify you by race in Philadelphia.") She wishes for his abilities and "talents to come through so a teacher will develop it." She wants someone "to sit down with him and teach him the basic essentials," but basically these essentials should be "reasons to draw upon life experience." She feels that talents "come out of life experience."

Helen is "seriously thinking about daycare and will investigate possibilities." She feels that she is "qualification conscious" and "wants to make sure she knows what they're doing; such as, who and what and how they're dealing with kids." She doesn't want anyone to "just sit him in front of a television all day." She feels that "people contact is important for a child's development and that daycare helps a child begin outside world development." In general, she believes, daycare "has a lot of advantages for working mothers and school mothers, that it gives a kid a father, that it gives the mother an opportunity to lead her own life as a child leads his." She thinks that daycare "went through a fad; everyone wanted their child in daycare." Since then, it has "turned down and people are seeing good things about daycare. It's just a matter of the parent feeling good about the right care." In addition, Helen prefers that the center be as "close to home as possible." Finally, as far a future schooling is concerned, Helen wants her son to finish high school.

FUTURE RELATIONSHIPS

Helen Jones feels that she is "doing good on my own." She further says that she is "not going to deny that I wish sometimes that there were a man around to let me fall to pieces sometimes." She is cautious about men. She thinks that there are a "lot of men around who are a lot of bullshit." She is "tired of lines," and wants "security." Nevertheless, she doesn't want a "permanent re-involvement." She is "not ready for that." She would really like to be with men, but the men she's been with she's glad she's without. Generally, men, she feels just "want to get into bed." She "needs more than that." She thinks that she'll become re-involved sometime ("It'll happen one day") but she's cautious about who and why. ("People get involved for the wrong reasons.") She says that a man once told her that she was his property. She replied that she was not a "piece of furniture that you move here and there." She wants respect and feels a lot of men are not willing to do that. ("There are not many men liberated out there.") She says she "teases a little, but leaves men alone." She is particularly not concerned about getting involved with a man because her son requires a male presence. She doesn't think that the absence of a father will take away from her son's masculinity. Furthmore, Helen feels that she can turn to her son's godfather for support.

CONCEPTIONS OF IDEAL FAMILY LIFE

Helen Jones says that she has never sat down and thought of the "ideal" family life for herself. She has fantasized about "having a good man around who could share both of us, love both of us." She wishes for an "emotionally strong man." ("We all have to fall apart sometimes; I need someone around to put me back together again.") However, she has "no conception of perfectness" ("Perfect for me?") and certainly does not see herself in an "ideal family situation." After much concentration, she added that what would be nice for her would be to "live with a man in an apartment or house and be together while we still are ourselves." She doesn't think a man should be the "sole supporter," and doesn't want to stay home herself and be "stagnated like those women who wait 'till their kids go to college and they have nothing." She feels that two people can "stay together as a family unit and be together and still be independent while supporting each other."

RACISM

Helen Jones feels that she has "never really encountered racism." She calls herself laughingly a "half breed" because her biological mother was white and her father black. She feels that she has been and "will always be considered as black." Helen says that "color is a secondary thing" to her; she has "learned to look away from a person's color" and doesn't "associate with people who look at color." She thinks that all people are basically the same physically and that it is a waste of time to look for differences. She does not like black militants. She thinks that they should just "be themselves" and not "condemn" her. A black militant once told her that she was "too black for the whites and too white for the blacks. When the revolution comes, no one is going to want you." Helen replied that "when it's all over, I'll be able to get foreign aid better than you."

Helen is raising her son, she says, "without a color attitude." She feels that he has "two cultures open to him and that the final decision is up to him." ("If he wants to take a Black Studies course, I'll encourage him.") Helen finds it "easier to relate to both sides." She says that she has an "understanding of the white man and his warped mind and an understanding of the black." Concerning her own upbringing, Helen felt that she was "always a person — neither black nor white — but when I was in school, people treated me like a black person." There were no handicaps in being black per se; she says that in her community, it was not a racial thing, but a money thing; who had money made a difference. On the streets, as an adolescent, Helen felt that she was treated "just like a kid on the street. We saw each other as people." She has never felt any discrimination "except when travelling through the South where bigotry is obvious." She says that most of her friends today are white because "people I choose as friends think like I do. We can communicate."

ATTITUDES TOWARD BEING A SINGLE PARENT

A primary asset of single parenthood, says Helen Jones, is that she used to think about being a mother and father to her son, "but not anymore." There is "no real role playing." She does not worry about "the mother-father image." She is the "chief authority figure to her son and treats him like a little human being. We are real close and have a good relationship. A parent, I am. My son calls me 'mamma.' It's just a label." Being a single parent, says Helen, allows one to get away from roles.

A primary liability of single parenthood, she insists, is that "it has its moments when I wish I could push him OFF." But there are "good moments when he comes at me with his arms outstretched and we hug." She feels she has control over her son's life but is more "like a guide to him." She likes the idea of teaching him "morals, impressing him on how he can live his life when he becomes a man." She does not consider herself a "strict mother," and doesn't feel an "obligation about raising him, teaching him." She feels great pleasure in single parenthood because "it's a learning experience."

SINGLE-PARENT FAMILY NEEDS

The strongest need for single parents, Helen Jones feels, is a supportive group "to see us through dealing with crisis, to relate to each other. We are not free of our anger and frustration." She thinks that single parents are a "highly segregated group" that is stigmatized: "When I go into the hospital with my son they want to know my marital status. I say I'm single. They have a way of looking at you to try to put you down. I look right back and say, 'IS THERE SOMETHING WRONG?' " Helen does not know of any group or organizations for single parents. She thinks that "single parents are a group of loners who need each other's support," particularly around "basic common problems like discipline, child rearing, school. I get confused about what I'm going to do next." She thinks that single parents "find themselves with a lot of restrictions — most are on welfare — and it's important to support one another concerning these restrictions."

Helen says that "when I announced to the world that I was going to have a child, people turned away. I felt a sense of abandonment." She told herself that if she was "not going to get accepted by family, then she needed friends." She feels, in a way, "stigmatized and weird." She wants a "true sense of acceptance among peers," but family and friends "say one thing and feel another." She feels that "tradition and society have always impressed on people that a woman with a child alone has fallen off the line." She gets the feeling that people look at her son as just another illegitimate child. She responds by looking straight into their eyes and saying, "I am a single woman with a child. I don't really give a good holy fuck what you think. You can shove it up your ass and sit down on it." She adds, "I can look down my nose as good as anyone else. I'm just as good as the next person." She says that most black single parents she knows are "not married and most whites are widowed or divorced or separated." She thinks that there is much more acceptance by society of a single parent who has been married. But Helen feels that she's seen "too many fucked-up marriages and I say that I don't want that for my child. It messes kids' heads. If I believed in the institution of marriage, I'd be married. I believe firmly in being a single parent. I don't think that I should go out and get married because society says so."

HARD TIMES AND HOPE
William A. Mason

The Simmons family: Mother: Alice; Cheryl Jackson, 23, and her 2-month-old daughter; Debra Marshall, 28, divorced; Sara Berwell, 24, separated and out of the household; Denise, 20.

Except for Sara, the Simmons family share a five-bedroom apartment in Roxbury, Massachusetts. Mr. Simmons moved out eight years ago and has since remarried, has a 4-year-old son, and now lives in Dorchester. The Simmonses live as a family with the older siblings providing income through odd jobs and money offered every now and then by their husbands. Alice, the mother, receives welfare. They seemed to be "chummy" with their neighbors, and frequent the neighborhood bars and watch television for entertainment.

Mrs. Simmons has a ninth-grade education and Mr. Simmons attended school through the seventh grade. He worked in numerous low-paying jobs — dock hand, janitor, etc. Mrs. Simmons didn't offer information about the separation other than to say it never seemed to work out easily. I suspect ongoing frictions initiated by Mrs. Simmons' liking to go out led to the divorce. Mrs. Simmons had high hopes for "her girls" but stated, "I let them lead their own lives. As long as I have a home they do too!"

The family was referred to the mental health unit because Denise, 20, had been arrested five times for boosting (shoplifting). Mrs. Simmons suggested that she didn't support or condone Denise's activities because since Denise was the baby "she never wanted for anything."

Because Denise was the focus for the family's being at the Mental Health Center, the family is described in terms of her problems and aspirations. She is of average height and weight, fairly attractive with long hair and slightly crooked teeth. She is a senior at a neighboring high school completing all the required nursing courses, and expects to graduate in June. Denise wants to go on to college and become a registered nurse. She has a high interest in interpretive dance and even took tapdancing lessons. Mrs. Simmons has encouraged her goals. Denise says that she "boosted" only because "she likes pretty things." Her sisters all had similar goals of finishing school but early marriages and pregnancies thwarted these goals.

Mrs. Simmons suggested that she has always promoted independence for her girls; that way, "if anything happens to me they can survive." She laments that Denise's behavior problems might be caused by spoiling her and is banking on Denise as the one "to make something of herself."

Information sources for the family include bar talk, chats with neighbors, *Jet*, the evening news. Because of limited funds, television viewing is heavily weighted, and in many cases is the real family gathering time. Meals are taken at different times except for Sundays and holidays. Community activities and involvement is limited, although Mrs. Simmons has visited the high school, courts, and the mental health unit because of Denise's run-in with the law. There seems to be no ongoing practice of religion except for observance of holidays — Easter and Christmas. All members have voted in elections when friends and neighborhood workers encourage them to do so through voter registration campaigns, and when black candidates are in the race.

HERE TODAY, GONE TOMORROW
Nanalee Raphael

Mrs. Eleanor Harris' family lived on the top floor of a four-story building. The apartment was clean and had a comfortable, "lived-in" appearance. Stacks of 45 rpm records lined the top of the floor-standing stereo. The living-dining area was tastefully decorated and had a gilt-edged mirror and two inexpensive ceramic flower decorations hung on the wall. Mrs. Harris and I sat down to talk in a small room off the living room, a bedroom which was furnished as a sitting room with a second television (there was another in the living room), a heavy mock leather couch, and a couple of end tables.

As we talked, Mrs. Harris often interrupted the interview to speak with her daughters. Among the many requests, she asked them to start the dinner, turn over the rug, take a dress to the cleaners, or go out and purchase a recently released record. Peggy, the younger daughter, who had not quite lost all of her "baby fat," prepared a cup of coffee for her mother. Mrs. Harris then reminded Patricia, the older daughter, that she was not to go anyplace that evening because she told a lie the day before.

Mrs. Harris was born in Georgia. She was the oldest of four siblings. Of her childhood and youth she said, "I didn't have to work my way through school. I didn't do babysitting or jobs like that. My parents gave me the money I needed, even after I left school." She said that her parents were above the poverty level and that she and the other family members had good clothes and a decent home. Mrs. Harris' family moved North to New York State when she was less than one year old.

Her father had a grade-school education only, but her mother enrolled in several courses at the college level. Mrs. Harris remembers her mother as the person who checked her homework and encouraged her to get good grades. Despite such encouragement, Mrs. Harris dropped out of high school after the ninth grade. Since then, she has taken some night-school

149

courses but has not received a high school diploma. Her enrollment in such courses is not continuous, although she states that
she eventually hopes to obtain the equivalent of a high school
diploma.

In Albany, Mrs. Harris met her husband and married
when she was 16 years old. Within a period of three years, she
gave birth to two daughters. Shortly after the birth of the second
child, Mr. and Mrs. Harris were separated. Three years later
they were divorced and Mrs. Harris has provided for her
children alone for several years. After the divorce, Mrs. Harris
moved to the apartment in which she now lives.

Mrs. Harris works for a federally funded community action program as assistant coordinator. Before affiliating with
the community action program, she worked for an electrical
firm but was laid off because of absenteeism due to a bout with
bronchitis. Her work with the community action program
began on a part-time basis as a community aide. In that role, she
arranged community meetings for discussion of problems and
conducted door-to-door casework surveys. After about a
month of part-time work, Mrs. Harris decided to apply for the
assistant coordinator position. "I got it," she said, "because they
liked the way I acted and the way I presented myself." Now her
work includes helping people find jobs appropriate to their
skills, helping poor families settle rent and welfare problems,
referring people for job training, and helping families relocate
when their living units are condemned.

Concerning her personal life, Mrs. Harris said, "I like to
travel. When the girls were younger, I lived in California for a
year. They stayed with my parents and I moved all over — Los
Angeles, San Francisco, all around California. I went to Greece
for three weeks for a vacation once. That was real nice." Mrs.
Harris noted that she still would be young when her 11-year old
and 13-year old finished school. Then, she said, "I'll go back to
traveling. I like being independent."

Regarding her children's education, Mrs. Harris said, "If
they want to go to college, I'll give them money to pay for their
first year but after that they're on their own. If they want to
travel, I'll give them money for that after they graduate. I don't

push schooling on them. I think it's a waste of money. But I tell them if they want to do more than their mother, they need better training."

Mrs. Harris reflected on her role as a disciplinarian and offered this opinion of herself: "I'd say I'm stricter with my girls than my parents were with me. I don't think I was spanked enough. When I say 'no' I mean 'no'! Oh, yes, I spank the girls when they're bad. I'm in favor of punishment when it's needed. I don't mind them being punished in school, either, if they deserve it."

Mrs. Harris is not pleased with her housing. She explained that there are a number of people in her building who receive public welfare and that she does not like this because, as she sees it, "They let the place run down and don't take care of their kids very good. I guess I shouldn't talk, really. I was on welfare once, but I'm off now. There are a lot of working mothers in this housing development."

Mrs. Harris thinks the neighborhood in which she lives is "pretty good," but she is not quite sure. She said, "There are a lot of Jews, and it's racially mixed; but there isn't any recreation for the children." She is more favorably impressed by the neighborhoods on the East Side. "They are really nice and well off," she observed.

The girls attend different schools. Patricia walks to the junior high school each morning and Peggy takes the bus to her elementary school. Peggy is in the sixth grade and Patricia is in the seventh. Patricia started school a year late.

This is the household afternoon and evening routine. The girls have to do their homework before they watch TV or play. "I don't check their homework, but I can tell if they've been working by their report card marks. If they have a lot of work to do, they let me know and then they don't have to help with chores. I have never gotten any bad reports from school about their work." When the girls have school work to do, they sit at the dining room table or in the sitting room. Peggy usually finishes her work in school; she has few homework assignments. Patricia was able to do school work beyond her class level and could have skipped a grade but Mrs. Harris decided that it was better that she continued in a class with kids her own age.

Mrs. Harris described her household of three as "real close." No one has ever been in trouble with the police, and the children are getting along very well in school.

Although Mrs. Harris was raised a Baptist, she seldom attends church and hasn't brought her girls up with any religious preference. "Sometimes the girls go to the Episcopal church near here," Mrs. Harris said. "I go when I feel like it, I guess. If I don't go during the rest of the year, I certainly don't go on Christmas or Easter."

Mrs. Harris has a boyfriend, Bob, whose son Wayne (age fourteen) stays with the Harris family when Bob has to go out of town on sales trips. "The girls get along with Wayne real well, like brother and sisters. Sometimes when we have a date, the girls babysit with Wayne but not all the time."

Mrs. Harris usually disciplines Patricia and Peggy, although Bob and Mrs. Harris' parents often help in this respect. "Their grandparents are always teaching them manners. But they spoiled them for awhile. They were the only grandchildren for a long time."

The family has dinner around 5:30 or 6:00 each evening. "I cook for two days usually, so we have leftovers every other day. The girls fix after-school snacks themselves when they get home if they're hungry," said Mrs. Harris. Breakfast is an individual affair. Each family member prepares her own. On weekends the family members eat lunch together.

During the week Mrs. Harris awakens first at 7:00 a.m. Peggy gets up in time to catch her bus for school at 8:00 a.m. Patricia's school day ends at 2:45 p.m. She comes home and plays inside until Mrs. Harris returns from work at 5:30 p.m. Peggy gets home from school around 3:30 and plays with friends until dinnertime. Evenings are spent doing homework and watching TV, except on Tuesdays, which is the evening on which the family bowls.

Mrs. Harris sleeps in until 11:00 a.m. on weekends. But the girls get up around 9:30 a.m. and shop or visit with their grandparents. In the afternoon, on weekends, Mrs. Harris shops or cleans, Peggy goes to the movies, and Patricia plays inside. Dinner is a little earlier, around 4:30 or 5:00. After-dinner activities include TV, visiting, or finishing the cleaning of the apartment.

"I live above my means, I know," Mrs. Harris said when asked if she had problems making ends meet. Her monthly rent on the apartment takes about half of her monthly income. Bob, her boyfriend, helps pay the rent.

The apartment is relatively large. It has a kitchen, three bedrooms, a living room and dining room, two bathrooms, and an outside balcony. The family has three televisions, several radios, and a phone with an extension in the sitting room. "This is a convenient location," said Mrs. Harris. "There is a shopping center and the bus line runs right past us."

Mrs. Harris returned to a theme discussed earlier that the neighborhood is "going down." "No upkeep," she said. "All these welfare people don't try to get better. There's alot of litter and destruction. And all the large families. I don't think there should be more than three kids to a family. Oh, yes I thought about moving. It's not worth what I'm paying in rent. I'd like to move to the East Side." When Mrs. Harris referred to her neighborhood she was thinking in terms of the five apartment buildings in her housing complex.

She knows about five families in the housing complex. She believes the police do a fine job of enforcing the law, since there are no real problems in the area. "This isn't a real dangerous area, but it isn't a real safe one either. I guess it's about average. If I could I'd have a place for kids here, to keep them off the streets. A recreation center instead of all the grass, a playhouse."

If she encountered problems, Mrs. Harris would turn to her parents or to Bob for help. "I'm closest to them," she explained. "It would have to be money problems, because I can handle all the others."

"Pat, what kinds of chores do you and Peggy have to do for your mother?" the interviewer asked one of the children. "Oh, we mostly have to clean and straightens up; then on Sunday we switch off. We don't need a reason for it, but it helps us if we do. If we don't finish our chores, we have to stay in. One day last week I couldn't go out 'cuz I said I finished and Mama found out that I didn't.

"Peggy and I get along O.K. We argue alot ... mostly over clothes.

"I like school once in a while. If I had another choice, I'd like to travel. Math is my best subject, then English and then gym. I don't like social studies. I don't like to flatter my teacher and she likes to be flattered. There are only two black kids in my class — me and another girl. Other kids can flatter the teacher but I won't. I hurt her once when I read a poem I wrote at an assembly. I didn't mean to and I told her later. It was about who I really respect and I respect Lincoln, not her, but that's the way I feel.

"I want to be a singer or a math teacher. I guess I'll need about four years of college to be a teacher. I'm a real good singer; I've been in a lot of talent shows, sometimes with a band and sometimes just singing to records. I love to sing. Oh, no, I don't want to act, that's just ... yecch." Patricia shriveled up her shoulders, stuck out her tongue, and made a face clearly expressing her distaste for the idea.

She got up and moved around quickly as she continued talking. "I don't want to be a singer all my life. I want something to fall back on, that's why I'd like to be a teacher. I s'pose I could sing until I was about thirty and then teach. I want respect for myself and partly for my race. I want friends who respect me for being myself."

Patricia thought for a while but couldn't find an answer to the question, "What kinds of things are good to have?" In the negative sense she answered that envy was bad. "When people are jealous of you it makes it bad for you. The best think that ever happened to me? ... well, winning awards like in the talent contests."

Patricia enjoys traveling and under a summer program sponsored by a local organization went to Canada. "I got to dance onstage with Sam & Dave (a popular rock band). A bunch of girls were dancing on the side and they pulled me onstage and I danced for about three songs up there. They wanted me to stay to talk with them after, but I got a little scared (giggles here) and we all got out of there. I have been to New York three times. I don't like it, except for clothes. Other than clothes, it hasn't got anything. Don't see how people can live there. Nothing bad ever happened to me, just good things. I guess I've been pretty lucky."

Patricia's interests reflected the fact that she is still 13, barely a teenager. She likes to sing most of all and can accompany herself on the piano. When she's with friends she likes to talk, play cards or Monopoly, or watch TV. She's scared of dogs but likes puppies. And if she had three wishes she'd wish for clothes, a car, and to be a singer, in that order. "I don't want to wish for money. I don't want everything. If you get everything, then what's the use of living?

"I'm not going to get married until I'm thirty-nine, and have one child. I hope it'd be a little girl. I like to comb their hair. If I have it before I'm married, I hope it's while I'm young, like Mama. She's only twenty-eight you know. She had me when she was fifteen and her parents took care of us until she got married when she was sixteen. I like little kids. During the summer I worked as a babysitter. It was a real good job; I got paid real well. I kept half and gave half to Mama before she asked for it. She gives me money all the time, so I figured I could give her some. I didn't need all that. Yep, I like to hold children and play with them."

Mrs. Harris felt her mother influenced the girls most in finding part-time work (which Mrs. Harris preferred the girls not do) and helping the girls with homework. Everyone, including grandparents and aunts and uncles, had some form of influence in teaching the girls manners. "I let the girls decide what they want to do when they grow up, though. We talk about different jobs, but they're the ones who are going to decide. I don't decide where they go to school; the Board of Education does that. They make their own choice of church, although their grandmother wants them to stay Baptist. If I buy a car, I know what kind I want even though everyone else tells me what kind I should have. Number of children? That's up to me, if I make a mistake, then it's up to nature."

Mrs. Harris does not belong to any organizations,

although she has been a member of a church choir, has helped with girls' club activities. Informally she socializes with her co-workers. Her daughters belong to a young people's group at the Episcopal Church, a school-connected girls' club, and the track team. She was vague and did not have specific knowledge about her girls' activities.

Mrs. Harris was unable to describe her family's attitude about the civil rights movement. None of the family has even participated in a demonstration, or has been discriminated against in the way of employment. "I really don't know much about it. Whichever way these college students want it is all right with me. It really doesn't faze me."

Besides bowling together, the family sometimes attends concerts and plays. The girls enjoy going to concerts, whether they're classical or rock. And as Mrs. Harris' younger brother and sister are all in Albany with their families, there is much family interaction. "We have reunions or get together on special holidays or just get together at my parents'."

Patricia and Peggy don't see their father often, but they do know who he is. Mrs. Harris feels that the girls are very fond of Bob, her boyfriend, and are more apt to respect him that their father. Not only does Bob help support the girls by helping to pay the rent, but also treats them by buying presents and taking them out. As Mrs. Harris sees Bob three or four times a week, the girls are also in contact with him often.

Mrs. Harris finds her present job exciting and at the moment is not interested in moving on to something else. "But if I get tired of it, I'll just quit and go somewhere else," she finished laughingly.

FAITH AND ENDURANCE
Donna Willey Schum

It was a somewhat rundown neighborhood and I was very nervous. The first door I went to was opened by a shy, well-dressed little girl with her fingers in her mouth. I asked if I could possibly speak to her mother and she led me up some stairs and into a large apartment with what seemed like a whole living room full of clean, neatly-dressed children. I repeated my question and stood awkwardly for a moment until an older child asked me to sit down and left the room, returning with an older, rather weathered-looking woman.

At first Mrs. Fisher and I had trouble understanding each other. The first few questions had to be explained and repeated; finally the conversation became so confused that the oldest child (the children were all lined up on an enormous sofa gaping at me) began to do a bit of interpreting until we were genuinely communicating ideas. It was difficult to entirely fill out the interview forms because Mrs. Fisher did not want to discuss some things. Consequently, I did not press her to strictly adhere to the interview sheets. I was learning a great deal about the family by just letting her talk.

Mr. Richard Fisher and his wife, Mrs. Gladys Fisher, have been married for twenty-eight years and have had eight children of their own, one of whom is still living at home. The others are all married and have families of their own. One son works for Ford Motors, two are roofing specialists, two are ministers of their own churches, and the youngest son is currently unemployed; and as Mrs. Fisher told me, he is the only one who was ever a discipline problem and had slight trouble with police. Of the two daughters, the oldest one is now working her way through college to become a physical therapist, and the younger, who is still at home, works at a neighborhood health center as a dental hygienist. Almost all of the children live in the same neighborhood with their families and Mrs. Fisher babysits

157

for eight grandchildren every week-day while the parents work, and sometimes nights and weekends also. These grandchildren range in age from two to teenage and appear to be thriving. Also, a short time ago, Mr. and Mrs. Fisher took two foster children into their home to raise; Thomas, who is six, and Henry, who is fifteen. In spite of their ages, which Mrs. Fisher refused to tell me, Mr. and Mrs. Fisher are still active parents and loving every moment of it.

Mr. Fisher is from Alabama and Mrs. Fisher is from Georgia, where they met and raised their family, until twelve years ago when they moved directly to Rochester to join their older daughter, who had already lived there six years. One son lives in Florida and is the only one of their children that the Fishers do not see every day.

The family income is below the poverty line. Mr. Fisher has been unemployed for four months. Mrs. Fisher probably did not include in the family income the allowances that she probably receives for the two foster children and funds she gets for babysitting the grandchildren. She did not respond readily to these questions. and she was not at all specific. Mr. Fisher was formerly employed in a bakery for some time. Mrs. Fisher would not tell me how much education she and her husband had, because she said it was too little to mean anything. She seemed to be ashamed of the level of schooling which she had completed. Shirley, their twenty-four-year-old daughter who still lives with her parents, completed high school and attended a training program of some kind for her work as a dental hygienist. Six-year-old Thomas has completed first grade and fifteen-year-old Henry has completed eighth grade, and has a tutor in addition to school.

This family is obviously very close, and has very strong family ties. Mrs. Fisher says that the children never had trouble with the police and all are doing or did very well in school. She does most of the disciplining herself mainly because Mr. Fisher usually works long hours when he is employed. They make all important decisions together. Both help with homework and with teaching and training the children to be "decent people," considered by the couple to be very important functions of child-raising, which they are tremendously devoted to.

Regular meals are planned and prepared by Mrs. Fisher. She gives her family and grandchildren breakfast at 7:00 (their mothers leave early for work), lunch at noon, and dinner for her family at 6:00. All members of the family usually eat together, except when Mr. Fisher is absent for lunch because of his working or looking for work. Mrs. Fisher would not even begin to tell me schedules of her family for certain days. She said the older ones mainly work and go to church and the children play, help out around the apartment, and go to school.

The children do not have any specific time set aside for homework, but Mr. and Mrs. Fisher make sure that it gets done. She feels that the children will form a bad attitude towards school if they are forced to do schoolwork when they would rather do something else. They are learning independence by organizing their own free time. Homework is usually done in the children's room. No one in the household has visited the school this past school year because Mrs. Fisher babysits all the time and Mr. Fisher is usually working. Teachers and school officials do not visit, Mrs. Fisher thinks, because the children behave so well in school.

The foster children have a case worker who visits regularly, and Henry has a special tutor who visits — a white student from a local college who works with emotionally disturbed children. Mrs. Fisher told me that Henry came from a depraved and wretched environment, and that this "home life" had left its mark on the fifteen-year-old's sensitive mind. He needs special care and Mrs. Fisher is confident she can give him the love and attention he needs. He already seems to be responding positively to Mr. and Mrs. Fisher and the other children. He's very creative and he does very well in most schoolwork, but he has social problems. His sister also visits him once a week. Six-year-old Thomas also had a difficult home life, but he has not been affected as much by it and he has almost completely accepted his new loving family in the two months he has been there.

Mrs. Fisher says the children have many ideas of what they would like to be. The oldest grandchild, the teenager Carol, told me she would like to work with children in some way —

probably with retarded children. She handled the small children all the time I was there. Mrs. Fisher would like the children to do service work and have professional jobs, but she will let them decide as she did with her grown children. She had no idea how much education was needed for this type of work.

Mrs. Fisher is dissatisfied with her neighborhood only in the sense that she has a dream of living away from the city on a farm with her whole family and a lot of animals really "close to nature." She wants to enjoy God's creation as he created it. Her only thoughts of moving are in this context. She classified the neighborhood as white working-class. She feels the police do a fine job of enforcing the law in this area and it is quiet. She likes the idea of living in a white neighborhood because it is quieter and she enjoys the white students in the area, but she is uncertain of the reputation that the neighborhood has and she knows few people outside of her family. There is nothing she would like to change about her neighborhood.

The rented apartment occupied by the Fisher family has six rooms and a bath. What I saw of it was very attractive, nicely furnished, and neat. The front rooms were especially warm and cheerful. The family has three TVs in working order, many radios, and a telephone, which Mrs. Fisher feels she would be lost without. When in need of any help, Mr. and Mrs. Fisher contact members of their own close-knit family. They all depend on each other in tight situations, and most family members live in or near the same neighborhood — some even in the same apartment house.

Central and most important in the lives of the Fisher family is religion. Mrs. Fisher told me that they all try to go to church as often as possible, and that they also try to live their religion. "I got no education, but I know Jesus and that's all I need." Mrs. Fisher explained this by saying that she and her husband had been happily married for twenty-eight years and had raised many children with very little difficulty because they followed the "way of the Lord" and had felt the spiritual presence of Jesus, which kept them strong. She said their faith, and especially her faith (because others may be moved in different ways), gave her the insight and understanding needed to raise children, "for one surely needs more than physical comforts to fully develop youthful minds and hearts." The social life that Mr. and Mrs. Fisher have is centered around the church and they leave no time to be members of any other kind of organization or club. Their religion is a major binding force in the family and it is not the only, but the primary and most important tradition and activity that they share together as a family. It gives them strength to overcome difficulties. Of course, the children are involved in groups like Boy Scouts, sports teams, and clubs at school, but they are still actively involved in the church also. I do not believe the children resent this strict church attendance and involvement because it is so much a part of their family life.

Mrs. Fisher talked for quite some time about how she and her husband feel about raising children. She feels fulfilled in seeing them become decent people, strong in spirit and happy. She said that teaching and giving all the wisdom that Jesus gives her, to her children fulfills her as a person. She believes that the young generation of today should listen and attempt to learn from their elders, for with age comes experience and intuitive wisdom. Also, she said that the older people should stop complaining about the behavior of the young, and instead show that they have something to give and offer it. "In order for a child to develop in a family, one, as a parent, has to learn to communicate with that particular child and realize that he is a person and not just something to discipline. You must rspond to his sensitivities and discipline him accordingly, handling each child in a different way. "She said that a child knows if you recognize him as an individual and a person, and the way he develops is a result of the extent to which you allow him to grow and learn and be disciplined as that individual he is. "Parents who react to each child in the same way, see them as objects to be made into people in their own image, with their own standards. But children will not take to this and soon there is trouble."

Her foster child, Henry, who is mentally disturbed, needs very special care, she told me, but not so much that the other children think him more important than they. She and Mr. Fisher are slowly getting to know Henry and have already discovered certain areas which are extremely sensitive in his personality. They feel they are just beginning to reach him and are thrilled by it. Mrs. Fisher appeared to be a strict disciplinarian while I was there, but she made me realize that much more than strictness goes into raising children.

This family is certainly well adjusted to the problems and opportunities it has had to face in life. The atmosphere of the setting of the interview was warm, and this warmth semed to come from the love and companionship this family experienced in their life together. The fact theat Mr. Fisher had recently lost his dependable job, seemed to have little effect on their happiness, even though it probably upset family finances a great deal. Raising children is the most important thing in Mrs. Fisher's life, and though she does enjoy what physical comforts she has and misses those she does not have, I feel that even without this sort of economic security she would be really happy and contented just being with her family and being able to aid in the development of her children. I also feel that the whole family has probably seen much worse times and yet they were strong and close and have probably been so in their most difficult times. The lack of any family planning is not an accident, for Mr. and Mrs. Fisher do not believe in it, but their large number of children has not caused a lack of attention to any one of them. Also she seems to know how to handle a disturbed child intuitively and from experience. She and Mr. Fisher's lack of opportunity for more education has perhaps limited them to a lower-class status and a working-class neighborhood, but they have adjusted to this situation and have created strong binding family ties and warm happiness in their lives. I think their religion and their resulting spiritual happiness has played a great part in this adjustment. Also, the individual strength in the personalities of both Mr. and Mrs. Fisher has played a great part.

It does sound as though Mrs. Fisher has the more dominant personality, but I did not get the impression from my interview that she dominated her husband or family. She constantly spoke of the strength and help she received from Mr. Fisher and what a good man she had. She said there is none better, and his relatively quiet manner did not fool the children. They knew he could be stern if need be, and she felt that they looked to him for strength the same as she did. She insisted that any strength she had raising her children was due to the love and encouragement he gave to her. They make all the important decisions together and very seldom quarrel. The spiritual strength and binding family ties of this family have enabled it to face difficulties and the lack of opportunity in their lives. Hardships and good times have been shared, and knowing there is always someone to help out and depend on gives the Fisher family security and strength needed to meet any situation. In making their children "well-mannered, decent people," Mr. and Mrs. Fisher have given them strength of character and family values, making them better prepared to face possible difficulties and hardships in life than other children in perhaps higher-status levels.

LIKE MOTHER, LIKE DAUGHTER
Marshall T. Young

This black one-parent extended family consists of six members living in a five-room apartment house in the city of Watertown, New York. Mrs. Coreen Jones, thirty-one, is the mother of four children and is employed by a boarding school as a cleaning woman. Also living with the family is Mrs. Porter, fifty, who is Mrs. Jones' mother and grandmother to the children.

Mrs. Porter, the grandmother, was born in Alabama. She lived with her aunt and uncle, and eight brothers and sisters. The family later moved to Gerogia, where at nineteen she met and married Mr. Porter. Soon afterward Coreen was born. The Porter family moved to Watertown, where Mr. Porter found work in a local factory. Mrs. Porter stayed at home. During the next six years she gave birth to five children. Mr. Porter remained with the family off and on for ten years. The family moved about five different times within the Watertown area, each time moving because of rent difficulties. The family was once close but Mr. Porter had hard times finding employment; therefore he left the family after moving north. Mrs. Porter got some assistance from the Department of Public Welfare and later went to work as a seamstress.

The children attended the local schools for a while. Coreen quit high school in the tenth grade and went to work in a dairy. At age nineteen, she met Mr. Jones at a party and married him. Mrs. Porter was against the marriage, I presume mainly from her own experiences.

Mr. and Mrs. Jones moved to Cleveland, Ohio, where Mr. Jones was from originally. The marriage experienced many ups and downs. Mr. Jones was an unskilled laborer and at first found it hard to find employment. Mrs. Jones felt the family was "real close" for the first few years of marriage.

Despite the financial handicap after their first child

164

Michael was born, the family did manage to go out once a week. Mr. Jones' brother often gave the family small gifts to help relieve the burden. In the next four years Mrs. Jones had three children; a daughter, and twins.

Mrs. Jones said that around the time her daughter was born her husband started gambling and often got himself into trouble. The family then experienced great emotional distress. Mrs. Jones became ill and was forced to remain in bed for a period of two months.

Mrs. Jones tried but was unable to cope with the situation. Mr. and Mrs. Jones got a divorce and Mrs. Jones moved back to Watertown with her four children. She first tried to get an apartment but later moved in with her mother, Mr. Porter. Mrs. Jones' brothers and sisters were either married or in the armed service; so Mrs. Porter welcomed her daughter and the children gladly.

This extended family has remained together for four years. They have moved only once. The four children attend the local public schools, Mrs. Jones works for a boarding school, and Mrs. Porter works as a part-time maid in a private home.

Because Mrs. Jones works all week, the grandmother takes care of the children during the afternoons. Mrs. Jones tries to spend the evenings with the children, but she says she often just doesn't have the time. Mrs. Jones describes her family as close but because of her work schedule she is not able to be with the children enough.

Mrs. Jones has been dating a department store worker that she met three years ago through a mutual friend. She said that she didn't want to marry again but always smiles with the answer as if she really doesn't mean it.

Mrs. Jones likes her work, she says it isn't too hard. She quit once for a couple of weeks but decided to go back. She gave no explanation why.

The older child, her nine-year-old son Michael, often gets into trouble with the police and the school authorities. Mrs. Jones feels that he takes after his father. Mrs. Jones does not seem to respect Michael. She states that he will never hold a good job. She has no real idea of child-rearing methods that may help him to grow up without getting into trouble. Michael plays with what she refers to as "the gang."

Mrs. Jones has high aspirations for the rest of the children. She hopes the twins will become businessmen, but there is inadequate information about requirements for these vocations. She hopes the seven-year-old daughter will marry well and will not have to work.

The children are close except for Michael. He appears to resent the females in the family, especially his sister who does well in school. The twins, who are six years of age, are too young to really be expected to work hard according to Mrs. Jones. She states that she tries to teach them social manners.

Mrs. Jones has a boyfriend whom she calls Roy. He visits and plays with the children often. Mrs. Jones says that he teaches them games and that he also helps to discipline them. The children seem to like Roy very much. Michael is never around, however, when Roy visits, because of the amount of time he spends with his friends.

The family has few connections with community organizations, except for church, which the family attends regularly on Sunday. Going to church is a family affair; evern Michael attends Sunday school with thre rest of the children. The family does not actively participate in any civic groups or service groups. They have had contact with case work services because of Michael, but it has not been lasting or important to the family. Roy feels that within time he can help Michael.

Mrs. Jones has called this black neighborhood an average area and insists that all the children are well-behaved. She has no idea about the police activities or their competence. I sense a hint of resentment with reference to the police. This is probably a result of the problems that have arisen with Michael. She exhibits an apathetic feeling about social change and improvement. She would like to see a better playground area for her children and a cleaner neighborhood; yet she repeats that she has no time to get involved.

A very influential person in the family is the grandmother. She usually cares for the children, does the laundry, housework, and prepares meals. She teaches the children manners, etc. She helps supplement the family income. The family lives with an annual income right at the poverty line. This is sometimes aided by gifts from Roy.

When I asked Mrs. Jones if she has heard from Mr. Jones she only shrugged her shoulder and didn't answer. I am interpreting this as a positive reply yet I assume that it is only an occasional thing. Mrs. Jones has held many things to herself and cared not to disclose them. Although we were on very friendly terms, a few topics were awkward when mentioned.

I feel that this basically describes the Jones family. They are an extended family that, as of now, are not headed in any real direction. The mother and grandmother are not greatly involved with society. Mrs. Porter has her own set of friends whom she often visits. Mrs. Porter and Mrs. Jones have created their own world, and have produced a relatively stable situation. The family operates as a unit, except for Michael. At nine years of age, he is not a full participant and the family functions without him and does not know how to help him. This family has accepted Roy as if he were a member. The children and their grandmother hope that Mrs. Jones will marry Roy. The children often call him "father" and everyone seems to enjoy this, even Mrs. Porter. Mrs. Porter has mellowed over the years, according to Mrs. Jones. She no longer resents the institution of marriage and the indignities she has suffered.

YOUNG LOVERS AND STORM WARNINGS
Edward Sloan

The interview started at about seven o'clock in the evening and lasted to about ten o'clock. I happened upon the Butler home by chance, just by knocking on doors trying to get an interview. I was depressed and discouraged as I received rejections from several families that I had previously tried to interview. When I arrived at the Butler apartment, I was invited in. George Butler stopped watching television and Elizabeth Butler stopped washing the dishes and talked with me for three hours. Mr. Butler greeted me at the door. When I told him the reason for my visit, he called his wife and asked her to come to the door so that I could explain the class assignment to her. The generosity of the Butlers with their time greatly picked up my spirits. Mr. Butler assured me that he enjoyed the interview after it had ended. He and his wife invited me to visit them socially some time.

At first Mr. and Mrs. Butler were a little apprehensive; but after about twenty minutes, they became much more relaxed. Then, there was a very relaxed atmosphere. They made me feel comfortable and welcome. During the course of the interview Mrs. Butler served us coffee and home-made cookies. I must admit that her cookies were delicious.

While Mr. Butler appeared to be the dominant decision-maker for the family, one got the feeling that usually he consulted with his wife, as he did before I was granted the interview.

Mr. and Mrs. Butler had been married five years. Both were employed before marriage. She worked at an insurance company and he was employed in the stock room of a department store. Neither was explicit about the nature of his or her work. Mrs. Butler said, "When George Jr. was born I had to leave work to take care of the baby." Her mother and mother-in-law offered to take care of the baby so that she could continue working, but Mrs. Butler felt it was more important for a mother to stay home with her child and care for him properly. Mr. Butler agreed with his wife. However, he acknowledged, that it was more difficult, financially, to maintain an adequate standard of living after Mrs. Butler left her job.

Mr. Butler did not finish high school and he believes that this is one reason he has not been able to get a good job. So, the extra income of Mrs. Butler greatly helped the family.

Reduction in household income when Mrs. Butler stopped working was just the beginning of a series of overwhelming problems. George, Jr. was a premature baby and was not very healthy. Mr. Butler explained that the baby was in and out of the hospital for about four months during the first year. The specific illness of their first child was not labeled by the parents. Mrs. Butler simply described his problem this way: "the baby would just stop breathing sometimes."

Mr. Butler said that the constant care of the sick child made things very difficult for them. He missed work often to take the baby to the hospital. His boss became disturbed about the time away from work. As a result, "bad relations" developed between Mr. Butler and his supervisor. At the end of winter, after the Christmas rush, business was slow and Mr. Butler was discharged from his job. He believes that the bad relations had something to do with the fact that he was laid off rather than others who had worked for the company a shorter period of time. Mr. Butler had been employed for almost three years, compared with others who had worked for the company less than a year. At first Mr. Butler had "hard feelings" about losing a job. He has been looking for work but has found it difficult to obtain another job because business is slow and his education is limited. Mr. Butler is a member of the National Guard. He said it has a program which will enable him to get a high school equivalency diploma. He believes that he will be able to obtain a job and one better than the job he had before, after he gets a high school diploma. Mrs. Butler also believes that a high school equivalency diploma would greatly help her husband get a job. She is a high school graduate; but her husband quit because he had to help his parents support his family of orientation. He was the oldest son and had two younger sisters and one younger brother.

Mr. Butler has not worked since he was laid off from his stock room job. His family receives public welfare assistance which, according to Mr. Butler "is the only way we can survive until I can get a good job." Doctor bills for their son George, Jr., now almost two years old, and care for their newest arrival, a girl about two weeks old, were cited by Mr. Butler as pressing obligations, requiring public assistance, since he was out of work.

Both Mr. and Mrs. Butler are very proud of their children and look forward to raising them and providing a good home. In fact, their children appeared to be most important. Mrs. Butler asked me if I would like to see their children, and then she and her husband took me into the bedroom where they were. I was allowed to hold the baby. It was obvious that the parents were very proud of their little daughter. Meanwhile, Mr. Butler picked up their son to show me what a big boy he was. Clearly, these children meant more to Mr. and Mrs. Butler than anything else in the world. We then went back to the living room and the story of the Butler household continued to unfold. Mr. Butler said he did not feel right about being on welfare but that it was necessary for the time being in order to take care of his family. Even while working, it was difficult, he said, for the family to get by on his low wages. For this reason, Mr. Butler had pinned all hope on getting a high school diploma as a possible way of improving his earning capacity.

When I asked the Butlers how many children they were planning to have, both responded, saying, "Our family is large enough." They have a boy and a girl, and think that this is sufficient. They indicated that with a small family they could provide better things, a better home and an all-round-better life — perhaps the kind of life that neither Mr. nor Mrs. Butler had known.

The father in this household sees his life as one in which the odds have been against him; but he would like to send his children to college "so that they would have a better chance of being successful that I had." When asked what type of jobs they would like their children to have when they grow up, both parents felt that the final decision should be up to their children; but Mr. Butler added that he would like to see his son grow up to be a doctor or an engineer. In other words, he would like to see his son in a postion with a good future, one that would enable him to earn a good living. The parents would like their daughter to attend college also. They think that it is important for a girl to have an education and to be able to get a good job if ever the need should arise. Mrs. Butler added that she would like to see her daughter become a teacher. She believes that teaching is a good profession for a woman and is also a satisfying occupation. In terms of future plans for herself, Mrs. Butler said that when the children get older and go to school, she would like to go back to work.

The Butlers have a clean and neat apartment. It consists of a large bedroom and kitchen, a medium-sized living room and a bathroom. The furniture was a few years old but the Butlers had kept it in very good shape. Mrs. Butler said that since her husband is not working, he gives her a hand with the care of the babies and the housework.

The Butlers are not fond of the neighborhood in which they live, nor of the superintendent of the apartment building. "The undisciplined children who run around without parental guidance" was offered by the husband as a reason for not liking the neighborhood. "These children," he said, "are distrustful and have no regard for other people's property." He gave as an example the tires on his car that were slashed and the broken antenna. He assumed that these deeds were done by neighborhood children. Mr. Butler describes their neighborhood as one made up of working-class people with fairly large families. There are regular police patrols; but Mr. Butler feels that they really don't care too much about enforcing the law.

The family would like to move to a larger place. Mrs. Butler cites the need for more space now that they have the new baby. Mr. Butler would like to move outside of the city, where the children would have more room in which to grow up. He thinks it is good for children to grow up where they have room to play. There is a small yard where the Butlers presently live. Mr. Butler dreams of the time when he can be a home-owner. In his words, "I would like to have a place that is really mine." Despite these yearnings, both parents in the family agreed that they probably would miss the neighborhood in which they now live, if they moved. They like the location because it is close to everything, has a little grocery store a half block away. Also, they have some close friends who live in the neighborhood. They said that if they did move they still would get together with their friends, although they guessed that such gatherings might be less frequent than they now are.

Mr. and Mrs. Butler said they read the newspaper every day, read magazines, and watch the news on television. They think it very important to stay informed about the happenings in the world and community. They believe it would be even more important to be informed about the news when their children are older and start school so that they can talk with them about events and circumstances in which they are involved. Mrs. Butler is concerned about earning respect and trust from their children. She believes that this will come from talking intelligently with them and helping them with homework. She said, "It is very important for children to trust and respect their parents and not be afraid to ask for help when it is needed." The Butlers hope that their children will be as proud of them as they are of their offspring. They sincerely hope that they can be good parents and provide well for their children. One gets the feeling that their present circumstances have generated uncertainty as to whether these child-rearing goals can be accomplished.

After this phase of the conversation was over, I asked Mr. and Mrs. Butler if they were close to their families. They replied, "yes." Mrs. Butler said that they tried to see their parents at least once a week and visit them more often when possible. Mr. Butler said that his two sisters were married and living in the area and that they get together with them and their families from time to time. Mr. Butler's brother and Mrs. Butler's brother used to live nearby but have moved out of the area. They don't see them often now. Mr. Butler said that he especially enjoyed going fishing with his father. He said that this was very relaxing for him and he enjoys talking with his father. He explained that the relationship with their family was very close and that his father, on many occasions, had said that the family should turn to him if it ever needed any help. Mr. Butler did not indicate whether his father's family had been called on during this period of distress because of unemployment.

Although the Butlers would like to move into the country, they would prefer to stay in the region in which they now live. They have lived in this locality all their lives and "just liked it here." One reason may be that most of their friends and family are nearby. If they moved away, they would miss them greatly. Personal friends and family apparently are their greatest source of support, emotionally if not financially.

The Butlers are in their middle twenties but have done quite a bit of living and appear to be older than they are. An outstanding characteristic of this family is, the children come first and are the most important. It is fair to say that the primary goal in life of the husband and wife in this family is to provide a good home and be good parents to their children. All else is secondary. Whether or not this family can achieve its goal is problematical and depends on adaptations of the parents and on many circumstances beyond the control of the Butler household, such as educational requirements, employment possibilities, and welfare public policy. These are contingencies that must be considered in dealing with present problems and in planning future possibilities.

Part III

Black Families
And
White Families:
A Comparative Analysis

8 BLACK AND WHITE
AFFLUENT FAMILIES:
WHAT THEY CAN LEARN
FROM EACH OTHER

Despite their similar social locations, there may be different life-style variations between families of the majority and
of the minority. The working hypothesis of this chapter is this:
to be a middle-class or an affluent family is both an asset and a
liability, whether one is white and wonderful or black and
beautiful.

BLACK AFFLUENT FAMILIES

For the black affluent family, resisting racial oppression is
the overall mission that influences family organization and the
behavior of all family members. It is a common mission of all
black affluent families, and a mission held in common by all
family members. As such, it is a unifying experience for the
family. Thus, the chief source of unity of the black affluent
family originates outside the family. Black affluent families tend
to rally together to overcome the oppression of others.

The oppression of the society at large for black families is
manifested economically in terms of occupational and income
discrimination. Few black professionals are accountants, ar-
chitects, and engineers, lawyers, physicians, or dentists. Most
are medical technicians, or social, recreational, or religious
workers, or government workers, or teachers. Moreover, their
income reflects this fact. The median annual income for black
professionals is 20 percent less than that for whites. When
blacks have similar education and are employed in the same occupations as whites, there still tends to be a difference in in-

come, and the gap is unfavorable for blacks. All this has resulted in some affluent black families' believing that they have to be better than whites to achieve as much as do whites. Thus, for these families work is a consuming experience.

Despite rapid increases in educational achievement, few black middle-class adults are in managerial positions. It is fair to say that the number of blacks in charge of the establishments where they work is disproportionately low.

Thus an affluent black family tends to be pleased about the accomplishment of any member of the family. The accomplishments of all are exalted as an indication that "blacks are just as good as whites," which is a public posture. Privately, that same affluent black family tends to feel that it has to be better than whites because, the members claim, society in the United States today is racist and provides opportunities for blacks only after whites have been taken care of. Achievement among affluent blacks demands cooperation rather than competition within the family. It is true that family members do compete. But their competition is not with each other but with the dominant society, which they characterize as arbitrary and capricious in the way that it allocates opportunities and privileges. The accomplishment of any member, then, is used as evidence that all could do as well if the social system was not so oppressive. The fact may be that all members of a black household may not be able to achieve as well as one given member of that family. But black middle-class family members do not face this fact as long as discrimination persists. They lay all their problems at the door of racial discrimination, whereas majority group families tend to blame the victim for all problems, even those generated by the society and its systems. Minority group families tend to blame all problems on society and its systems, even those problems that individuals tend to create.

In the black middle-class family individual achievement is attributed to the collective effort of the family unit. For this reason, black middle-class family members shine in the reflected glory of any of their members — be it the achievement of father, mother, or child. They tend not to accept responsibility for the failures of individuals but claim credit for their successes.

Because the family works truly as a collective enterprise, all members try to prevent individual failure, if possible, by following a corporate kinship policy that guides and governs the behavior of each member. For example, whether or not a family member in the United States will obtain a college education or professional training is a family decision in the black middle class. The individual can resist. But the black middle-class family will persist and attempt to enforce its collective will.

Individualism and personal choice are secondary goals for the black middle-class family. Resisting racial oppression is of greater moment. Of discrimination the black middle class is constantly aware because its members are pushing against the boundaries that contain blacks; overcoming racial oppression is such a goal that all else must be subordinated to achieving it.

Affluent black families that draw upon any and all personal resources to overcome a racially discriminating society are both inner- and other-directed. The white society at large indirectly sets the goals of middle-class black family members because of the effects of racial discrimination. Instead of striving to become unique and antonomous individuals, family members are advised to turn aside from aberrant and novel behavior in favor of conformity to societal definitions of success. Black middle-class families tend to mold the lives of family members to meet the competition within the system on its own terms and to prevail by being as good as or better than others. They resist any form of discrimination but tend to conform to social expectation. Their inner direction strives to overcome the obstacles that others have given them. Their other direction causes them to expend much energy demonstrating that they can fulfill the existing standards and norms of society.

This orientation, then, limits spontaneity among middle-class black family members, particularly in their relationships with whites, and causes them to direct their energies to doing what whites do, with the expressed goal of doing it better. When reaction to the action of whites is the primary motivation for action, as it sometimes is, one could classify some middle-class black families as being obsessed with resisting racial discrimination.

Middle-class black families yearn for more association with other blacks so that their every move is not, as they believe, under scrutiny by whites. At the same time, they tend to be critical of other blacks who are more deeply rooted in the folk culture and its unique and different ways, for providing evidence that they believe whites use as reasons for excluding blacks from the privileges enjoyed by them. Thus, middle-class blacks are sometimes contradictory in their actions. They want to be near and apart from other blacks. They want to be near and apart from whites. These contradictions can cause strained relations within the black and the white communities of which these families are a part.

The fact that housing or residential integration has tended to lag behind other forms of desegregation in the nation may be, in part, a function of the racial discrimination of the society at large and also, in part, a function of the desire of middle-class blacks to have a place to retire to where they can "be themselves" and not be other-directed conformists.

The ways that affluent or middle-class black families have adapted to the society at large and their tendency to become obsessed with overcoming racial discrimination have had profound implications for interpersonal relationships within these families. What is sacrificed in terms of freedom to follow one's own desires and inclinations is compensated for by a collective or corporate effort in which husband and wife tend to work together as a team, often with both employed. In this connection the black middle class is more stationary, is less likely to move around geographically in search of new opportunities for the head of the household. Because of a tradition of dual employment the household is reluctant to pursue a new employment opportunity for one family member in a setting that may not provide an opportunity for employment for the spouse. A side benefit to their stationary existence is the building up of trusting relationships at work and in the community. Such relationships are one way of transcending discrimination.

The affluent black family is ingenious in its inner direction as it strives to overcome, and to cultivate those personal characteristics that will demonstrate qualification to be part of the system and to make that system work. Black middle-class family members are not so much concerned with the creation of new institutional systems as they are with being included in the existing systems and participating to the fullest as effective members. For this reason, middle-class black families are not very much concerned with overthrowing the existing system.

Success in the black middle class is measured in terms of "making it" in the existing system. Thus, the job title is as much valued as the job responsibility itself, and a high-ranking position in a predominantly white organization tends to be valued more than high status in a minority association. Becuase some middle-class blacks believe that they must be better than whites to achieve parity, they have fixated in an extraordinary way on eduction as the chief means of personal social mobility. Middle-class blacks who have achieved occupational parity with whites tend to outrank them in education.

The education route has been chosen by middle-class blacks because the opportunity for on-the-job experience has been denied to most blacks. With extraordinary educational preparation, some middle-class black family members have achieved occupational parity with whites so far as employment is concerned, but they still lag behind in terms of financial compensation. Thus, the dual income of husband and wife is required in some middle-class black families to maintain a middle-class style of life that whites are able to maintain with the earnings of only one worker in the household.

Finally, the home and the way it is outfitted has been used as another major indication of success. It is the haven to which all may contribute and is a sign to other minorities, if not to the majority, that the family has prevailed, that it can be done, that the family no longer is concerned on a daily basis only with survival. Even though the system as a whole may still resist the onslaught of middle-class black family members and continue to limit the extent of their participation in it, the home of the middle-class family is a sign that the family is on its way and will overcome some day.

WHITE AFFLUENT FAMILIES

The job of the head of the white affluent household is the major mission of the family. All else is subordinate to it. Continuity in school attendance by children, or resdence in a particular neighborhood, in a particular city, or in a particular region is less important than following the opportunities of employment for the head of the household. If the head is male, then work opportunities for the wife or whether the wife will work at all tend to be conditioned by the effect, or the perceived effect, of such activity on the advancement of the husband.

It is not irrelevant to say that some women in affluent white families are forced into idleness and are denied the creative outlet of work outside the home because of fear that employment of the wife and mother would jeopardize the family's social standing. This fear is beginning to pass away. Employment outside the home of white middle-class women in two-parent households has substantially increased so that one out of every two such women is gainfully at work. White women have now discovered what black women in the labor force have experienced for many years, that work is much more than just a way of making a living, that it is a means for realizing a sense of personal significance.

In the recent past, it had been the practice not permitting even the illness of other family members to interfere with the occupational success of the affluent, middle-class husband. The response of Rose Kennedy — wife of Joseph Kennedy Sr. and mother of nine children, including John F. Kennedy, former President of the United States — is indicative of how other family concerns are subordinate to the work responsibilities of the household's head in affluent white families. The *Boston Globe* asked Mrs. Kennedy this: "Your husband was away a lot. You never fought about or discussed whether he could spend more time at home?" Mrs. Kennedy answered:

No, I never would fight. He never felt that he had to get home. I think that's wrong. If I were ill, if I had a temperature, I would never tell him. If he went to California, I would never say, "I've got a temperature of 102," or "Joe Jr.'s got a temperature of 100" and have him worried. I never would think of that; I'd say it's a great day for golf, or it's a great day for the children to go sledding, or whatever it was. I think it's very selfish of women sometimes, either to demand or to be cross with their husband when he doesn't get home. I think probably then he hurries his business appointment or feels guilty about it. That I wouldn't do. I think that's selfishness on a woman's part. Of course, I was fortunate and the results came all the time. I mean, his business ventures in New York and Washington and California turned out to be very successful, so I had no reason to complain" (*Boston Globe* 1977).

The last sentence of this excerpt from Rose Kennedy's interview shoud be emphasized: " . . . his business ventures . . . turned out to be successful, so I had no reason to complain." The absence of wifely complaint is coupled with a linear accumulation of resources by the husband. In effect, the affluent white family has made a deal that has resulted in a rather rigid division of labor in the household. If the male head will make an extraordinary effort to provide resources for the physical well-being of the family, the wife will make an extraordinary effort to attend to his pleasure and not distract him with her personal concerns or those of the children. This fact has caused some women in middle-class white families to feel as if they were kept for specific purposes only.

By emphasizing the work of the husband as the major mission of the family, the middle-class white family is left without any unifying experience in which all may participate. Thus, the other members of the household are free to develop as they wish and to follow their own unique inclinations, with only one stipulation — that they must not interfere with the work of the father and the husband.

The offspring in affluent white households are free to receive or not to receive more education, to pursue or not to pursue an occupation, to be or not to be a part of the system. There is freedom to choose, to be original and spontaneous. This freedom provides the children in these families with multiple opportunities — opportunities to succeed and opportunities to fail.

Failure of a family member in the white middle class is rendered difficult, however, in an affluent household because of the presence of so many options and institutional supports. When failure does occur, society cannot be condemned because the father is among those in charge of society.

With no uniting mission to sustain joint efforts, the white middle-class family tends to be a collection of individuals who are united by where they live and what they should or should not do. They should not do anything to jeopardize the work of the husband and father, if the adult male is the head of the household; they should become autonomous and unique individuals. Because people other than members have limited access to it, the white middle-class family today has been protected from many of the imperialistic inclinations of other institutions and has not been forced to conform. Nonetheless, the geographic mobility required of many who wish to advance in business and industry still is an external experience to which many middle-class white families willingly adapt; so the white middle-class family has not excaped external authority completely.

Although middle-class white children and wives are free to follow their own inclinations if they do not interfere with the work of the father and husband, there are consequences that are most serious and that at times tend to pit family member against family member. For example, if the wife or child should not like society as it is currently organized and wishes to change it, the innovator must move against his or her own parent or spouse or against others in charge who are like the household head in one's own family.

Thus, the household that encourages freedom and independence on the part of its members may find the household members turned against each other in their public postures. This particularly is a threat between children and parents and between husband and wife. Quite often middle-class white youths who have been socialized in a setting of freedom and privilege do not wish to maintain society as it is. Conflict between them and their parents is an endemic possibility.

The husband and father in affluent or middle-class white families is given an almost impossible task of being the sole provider for the physical well-being of his family. Most white men in their moments of reality realize how vulnerable they are as individuals and immediately attempt to extend their strength through linkages with institutions. Thus they tend to measure their success in terms of their capacity to control institutions which, in turn, can help care for their family members. It is not enough to be a consumer. White middle-class adults must be producers; they must be in charge of social institutions as a way of guaranteeing their survival and capacity to do for their families what alone they cannot do.

The symbol of success of the white middle-class family, then, is the job of the husband and father and the power and authority that that job carries in society. Property and other material possessions are important insofar as they are indicators of power and authority. Power and authority connote a hierarchical arrangement of social organization. Thus, white middle-class families participate in groups, clubs, and other social arrangements that seek out people of similar kind and that exclude people who are different.

BLACK AND WHITE AFFLUENT FAMILIES: A COMPARISON

Comparison of similarities and differences between black and white middle-class families probably should begin with a focus on their mission. A family with a mission is better capable of establishing unity among its members than one without a mission. The probability is that in any population of middle-class families in the United States, more black than white families will experience unity. This is likely to be so because more white than black families probably are without an expressed mission that is a unifying experience. The privilege usually is that of affluent families to select a mission, and any number of missions may be chosen, or none may be chosen. But all affluent black families are confronted with the circumstance of racial discrimination. Overcoming this discrimination becomes their overriding mission. The black middle-class family, like the white middle-class family, may choose other missions.

But these usually will be of less significance than the mission that more or less is given to the black middle class, that of confronting racial discrimination.

It is beneficial for black middle-class families to choose missions in addition to race to keep the resistance of racial oppression from becoming an obsession. Regardless of their other interests, however, black middle-class families seldom can get away from race. Because of their achievement, members of the black middle class are constantly pushing against the boundaries of the castelike relations between the races in this society. It is almost impossible for one to be middle class and black in the United States and not to embrace the resistance of racial oppression as the major mission of one's family.

White middle-class families are free to choose their missions too. Most choose the occupational advancement of the father and the husband as the main mission of the family, around which all else revolves.

Black middle-class families could learn from white middle-class families the beneficial effects of permitting offspring the freedom to develop as they wish and to unfold as they are inclined. It is from such freedom that new systems and services for society are discovered. Spontaneity is the by-product of freedom. The inventive edge of black youth is often dulled by the parents, who program them to grow in a socially acceptable direction. Such conformity is for the sake of guaranteeing security in a known universe. Discovering the unknown is sacrificed when the freedom to explore is overcontrolled, as is frequently the case in the socialization of black middle-class youth.

The white female spouse could learn from the black female spouse the beneficial effects of a partnership in marriage. Not only have black middle-class wives and mothers contributed to the household income, they have also experienced a sense of power and participation in society. Because of their contribution, black middle-class mothers and wives are family decision-makers whose interests and concerns must be weighed and considered along with those of the husband and father. This arrangement of the black middle class could be followed by the white middle class. Then no one would feel kept or put upon as some middle class whites now feel. Some white families are beginning to establish genuine partnerships such as those that have characterized the black middle class for years.

Black middle-class families, more so than white middle-class families, emphasize self-reliance and self-determination. They do this because of their distrust of most of the institutions of society. They believe that none will give them a fair shake, that the cards are stacked against them, that they must make their own way. The coping characteristics of black middle-class family members are methods of enduring that could be taught to others and therefore, would be a contribution from middle-class blacks to whites and to the nation at large.

Recognition of the fragility of the individual and the need for institutional support systems to sustain people in time of need is an insight of white middle-class family members that should be shared with others. Particularly, blacks who rely almost solely upon themselves need to learn how to participate in institutional support systems that fulfill their own self-interests. Change within the individual is important, but change within the institution is more enduring. Moreover, institutions exist for the purpose of supporting individuals, who without their help may be vulnerable and ineffective.

When institutions are not available to stabilize the society, the white middle class creates them to deal with imbalance. Institutions are marvelous inventions, without which the individual would flounder. Few blacks have been responsible for the maintenance of institutions. Blacks have learned to distrust those systems of society that have oppressed them and have tended to turn away from participating in community institutions that could help them, because in the past many of these institutions were orgainzed against them and prevented the fulfillment of their own self-interests.

Individuals cannot do all that is necessary for their safety and security. Institutional systems must support them. Black middle-class families try to do on their own that which is inadequate and insufficient when attempted alone. They could learn from white middle-class families how to make, manage, and maintain social institutions that support and sustain individuals and protect them against difficulty and danger.

Both black and white middle-class families have some responsibilities that neither can share with the other, that are unique and characteristics of the minority or the majority. The black middle class is almost obsessed with race, for racial discrimination is an anomaly in a democracy, a gigantic national dilemma as well as a national disgrace. One could say that the black middle class, through court cases, complaints, and other activities, monitors the effectiveness of this democracy. Their actions, of course, fulfill their own self-interests, but they also are beneficial for other minorities and for whites, too, who believe in the rule of law. Always it is in the self-interest of the minority to maintain the procedures of democratic decision-making. Because all, including subpopulations of the majority, may be a minority at some period in time, the efforts of the black middle-class minority also benefit the majority.

Because the white middle-class majority controls the institutions of society, it has a responsibility to refine them, and to create new systems that are capable of fulfilling the self-interests of all, including members of the minority and of the majority. The responsibility of refining and creating new systems that are appropriate is uniquely that of a majority in a democracy, because only the majority has the power to implement a new arrangement; the minority has only the power to resist. When the majority does not fulfill its responsibility to create new systems and services for society, no others have the power to do so. White middle-class families should not shirk this responsibility. It is one that is uniquely their own.

In summary, this analysis has revealed that black middle-class families have solved some problems of living, with which the white middle-class families are struggling. And the white middle-class families have achieved some answers that remain as questions for the black middle class. Each group has something to teach the other, and each group has something to learn.

REFERENCES

Boston Globe. 1977. " A Conversation with Rose Kennedy." October 9.
Wilkes, Paul. 1977. *Six American Families.* New York: Seabury.

9 BOOTSTRAP UPWARD
MOBILITY

This exploratory study of a population in Washington,
D.C. analyzes (1) characteristics of employed poor blacks, and
(2) the differences, if any, between these characteristics and
those of working-class blacks who have pulled themselves out
of poverty by their own initiative and effort.

BACKGROUND OF THE STUDY

The employed poor and working-class households of this
study consist of 190 two-parent households whose employed
male spouses earned annual incomes below the official poverty
level. These households were located in the District of Columbia in an inner-city section in the northwest that consisted of 4
square miles, 18 census tracts, and 104,278 persons at the time
of the study. The area consisted of poor and affluent households
of both white and black racial composition. But it is predominantly a low-income working-class black area; 70 percent
of its population lives in census tracts in which the family median income is below the poverty line.

Information about the area's population was obtained in a
summer field survey. Approximatley 1,000 households were
randomly selected in 6 census tracts representative of the
various status levels in the area. Interviews of one hour's dura-
tion were conducted by residents of the area, who were
employed and trained to administer a schedule of questions
some of which dealt with economic problems.

To get an indication of how the employed poor might
climb out of the poverty into the working class, the 190
households with husbands of limited earning capacity were
divided into two groups: the total annual income for the

household was below the poverty line in one group and above it in the other group. Approximately 70 percent (or 133) of these low-earning male workers were in families with an annual family income below the poverty line, whereas 30 percent (or 57) had family incomes above this level and were classified as working class.

Working-class families climbed above the poverty level in spite of the limited earnings of the male spouse because of other sources of income. For this reason they are a good example of "bootstrap" upward mobility. This report is a comparative analysis between poor and working-class households to determine differentiating factors other than annual income of husbands, for these men had limited capacities in both kinds of families.

COMPARISON OF POOR AND
WORKING-CLASS FAMILIES

Of the 190 households in this study, 133 were below the poverty line, even though the husbands were employed; 93 percent of the husbands in these poor families were full-time employees and the remaining number were part-time workers. These statistics clearly are contrary to the myth that people are poor because they will not work. The employed men in the poor families tended to be young — one-fourth of them were under 30 years of age, compared with only one-eighth of the working-class men. All husbands were employed in similar jobs. About half in each group were service workers. There were few skilled workers — less than 7 percent in either group.

The families in both poor and working-class households had children ranging in age from infancy to 14 years. However, poor households had 38 percent of their child population under 5 years of age, compared with 24 percent of the child population among the working-class households. Another contrast was in the proportion of teenagers 15 to 19 years old — 27 percent in the working-class and only 11 percent in the poor households. Thus, employed fathers in poor households tended to be younger and their families tended to consist of a higher proportion of preschool children.

Working-class households were slightly larger, averaging 1 person more per household than poor families. In addition, there was a higher proportion of large households of 5 or 6 or more persons in working-class families. About 3 of every 10 working-class households could be classified as large, compared with approximately 2 of every 10 poor households. This was because a higher proportion of working-class households consisted of primary family members as well as relatives and nonkinsmen; 46 percent of the working-class, and only 27 percent of the poor, households included persons other than parents and children. Of the characteristics analyzed thus far, household composition is a major differentiator of poor from working-class families.

EMPLOYMENT OF THE WIVES

The most notable difference between the poor and the working class families had to do with the work of the wives. In the working-class, the wife was much more likely to be employed than was the wife in the poor household. Of wives in working-class families, 3 out of 4 were employed; slightly more than half were employed full time. The converse was true in the poor group. In poor families, 3 out of 4 wives were not gainfully employed. Possibly the presence of adults other than parents in the household is related to whether or not a mother with young children works. Also, there may be other factors associated with the higher proportion of working wives among the working-class families.

Most of the working-class employed wives were engaged in service work. Of the few wives in poor families who were gainfully employed, most were service workers too. However, the weekly income for employed women of the working class was higher than that for working wives in poor families. This may be because 7 of every 10 employed working-class wives rendered a service other than that of private household work, compared with 5 of every 10 employed poor wives. The weekly income of wives in working-class families was even higher than the limited weekly earnings of their employed husbands. The few working wives in poor families tended to earn less than their menfolk.

MULTIPLE WAGE EARNERS

The number of multiple wage earners in working-class families was increased not only by working wives but by the employment of relatives and other household members. For example, 3 or more members were gainfully employed in about 20 percent of the working-class households; only about 3 percent of the poor households had similar assistance. This means that most poor households had only one gainfully employed person of limited earning capacity. The working-class husbands had their low wages supplemented by the incomes of 1, 2, 3, 4, and in one instance 5 additional wage earners living in the same residence. The prevailing pattern, however, was 2 wage earners in the working-class family and 1 wage earner in the poor family.

The weekly earnings of husbands in poor and in working-class households were similar and so were the educational achievements. Of the poor, 36 percent, and 37 percent of the working-class husbands with limited earning capacity had only an elementary school education or less. Of husbands who had graduated from high school, the 42 percent in the working-class households was slightly larger than the 31 percent in poor households, but this difference is of little consequence in a sample of this size.

EDUCATION AS A FACTOR

A marked difference between poor and working-class households, however, was in the formal schooling of the female spouses; 46 percent of the wives in working-class households were high school graduates, compared with 27 percent among the poor.

Wives in working-class households also tended to be high

school graduates more often than their husbands. This may account for the fact that they also tended to earn as much or more than their husbands. In poor families, the earnings of the few working wives were less than those of their spouses, and these wives also tended to have less education than their husbands.

The ways of life of the Chandler and Butler families discussed in Part II are examples of households with fathers that have limited education and consequently limited earning capacities. Yet the Chandler family is working-class and the Butler family is poor. The difference between the social class level of these two families is due, largely, to the presence of multiple wage earners in one of them. The Chandler household consists of husband, wife and four offspring, together with the mother's sister and the wife of one of the sons. The father is a self-employed junkyard dealer and the mother, a part-time receptionist. By their own admission, the Chandlers have seen leaner times than they now experience. They have lifted themselves out of poverty by their own bootstraps, by pooling their meager resources. They could not experience the better life that they now live if the household depended solely on the father's income. The Butler family, consisting of father, mother and one child, is poor and receives public welfare. With an ill child, this nuclear household has no one to turn to for help, is struggling to make ends meet. The husband was a stockroom attendant but is out of work. The mother could not pick up the slack because the parents agreed that after the birth of their child, she would become a homemaker and not work. The Butlers are still young and with appropriate support eventually may be able to pull themselves out of poverty as the Chandlers have done.

This study demonstrates the value of multiple wage earners in poor families and indicates that more research is needed on the assets and liabilities of education and employment of the wife and mother in the household, especially the negative or positive impact of her work and formal education on the well-being of the total family.

Chapter 10

INTERGENERATIONAL
PROBLEMS OF POVERTY
FOR BLACKS AND
FOR WHITES

Several years ago, I conducted an ecological investigation of the distribution of a middle-sized city population by age and discovered that a "significant number of adults in all socio-economic areas move at least once in 20 years to a neighborhood of higher status." This finding indicated that a tendency toward upward mobility existed in all segments of the population (Willie 1960: 264). There seems to be a natural tendency for families and individual households to improve their circumstances in time.

Yet poverty has not been eliminated in the United States. Why the nation has been unable to eradicate poverty is an issue about which there is much conjecture. Some analysts argue that the upward social mobility described above was largely a function of the motivation, value orientation, and social organization of immigrant communities that fought their way up as ethnic groups from the bottom of the economic ladder (Glazer and Moynihan 1964). This same style of reasoning is used to explain why lower-class blacks remain impoverished. The circumstances of many black Americans are frequently explained as a function of the intergenerational transmission of poverty.

POVERTY AMONG BLACKS: Moynihan Thesis

In the United States Department of Labor report on *The Negro Family,* Daniel Patrick Moynihan maintained that "a national effort towards the problems of Negro Americans must be directed towards the question of family structure." He looked upon the weakness of the family structure as "the principal source of most of the aberrant, inadequate, or anti-social behavior that ... perpetuates the cycle of poverty and deprivation." He concluded that "the present tangle of pathology [among lower-class blacks] is capable of perpetuating itself" (U.S. Department of Labor 1965: 47, 30). In effect, Moynihan is saying that motivation, value orientation, and family organization of racial or ethnic group members contribute to the perpetuation or elimination of poverty within that population. The implication is that the family organization and cultural values of blacks differ from those of other ethnic groups and that these differences account for the persistence of poverty among the members of this racial category. This assertion has been advanced as a basis for social action as if it were supported by empirical evidence. In fact, assertions about the intergenerational transmission of poverty among blacks, such as Moynihan's, are inadequately documented.

TRENDS IN THE PROPORTION OF POOR PEOPLE IN THE TOTAL U.S POPULATION

The evidence shows that the population of the total United States population that is poor today is less than half of the proportion that was poor three or more decades ago. Clearly, some Americans have escaped the poverty that their parents experienced only one generation ago.

Research into the circumstances associated with poverty has not kept pace with policymaking needs because too many policy-makers have been more interested in justifying the presence or absence of poverty among "their people" rather than explaining it. Thus, the search for solutions to poverty has proceeded within the context of varying ideological orientations.

Moynihan has been identified with the hypothesis that poverty is perpetuated intergenerationally largely because of deficiencies in the family structure. In the United States Department of Labor report, he asserted that employment reflects educational achievement, which depends in large part on family stability (U.S. Department of Labor 1965). This trinitarian association however, must be understood for what it is — an assertion and not a conclusion based on evidence. In fact, the evidence appears to point in another direction.

Mollie Orshansky raised a serious question about the strength of the association assumed to exist between poverty and family instability when she pointed out that "two-thirds of all children in the families called poor do live in a home with a man at the head" and that "more than half of all poor families report that the head currently has a job." It would seem on the basis of the Orshansky analysis that many poor families are not unlike affluent families (Orshansky 1965).

POVERTY AND FAMILY CHARACTERISTICS

A study of income and welfare conducted by the Survey Research Center of the University of Michigan found that characteristics of parents did have a substantial effect on the amount of education their children completed, but that this effect accounted for less than half — 41 percent of the variance in years of school completed (Morgan et al. 1962: 383). The contribution of a combination of nonfamily factors to the amount of schooling received by children, therefore, was found to be more important than variables pertaining to the structure and process of the kinship system.

A Census report revealed that "six out of every ten college students in the United States were receiving higher education despite the fact that their fathers did not have this opportunity" (Miller 1964: 26). It is true that youth from higher-income families that have college-trained heads are more likely to complete school than are poorer youths. Yet it must be stated also that college youth come from all levels of American society. These data mean that no definitive answer is available concerning the extent to which insufficient education received by parents results in limited education and consequently low earning power for their children.

Because family characteristics have some association with the economic status of households, it might be helpful to consider characteristics that could have a significant intergenerational effect. The presence of one or both parents in the household is easily observed and usually is pounced upon as a quick and easy explanation. But because some low-income families are two-parent households, other variables should be considered too. A more subtle, but possible influential, variable is the education of the wife and mother in the family. The University of Michigan study discovered that "an average education attained by children is also influenced by the educational achievement of the mother. The more education the wife has relative to to her husband, the more education the children attain. ... Where the wife has less education than the head, achievement of the children is impeded but not so much as they are advanced when the wife has more education than the head" (Morgan 1962: 374-375).

PROMISCUITY, ILLEGITIMACY, AND POVERTY

Probably the behavior that has caught the attention of the public more than any other, and that is believed to be eminently responsible for the intergenerational transmission of poverty among blacks, is illegitimacy. The Department of Labor report authored by Moynihan stated that "the number of illegitimate children per 1,000 live births increased by 11 among whites during a period of two decades but by 68 among non-whites." The report further stated that of the million or more black illegitimate children in the nation most of them did not receive public welfare assistance. Nevertheless, illegitmacy was used as one of several indications of family breakdown among blacks that was assumed to be associated with the perpetuation of poverty. Why illegitmacy among whites was not declared to be a circumstance indicative of family breakdown was never clarified. The report stated that "the white family, despite many variants, remains a powerful agency not only for transmitting property from one generation to the next, but also for transmitting no less valuable contacts with the world of education and work. White children without fathers at least perceive all about them the pattern of men working. Black children without fathers flounder" (U.S. Department of Labor 1965: 8, 12, 34).

Again a series of assertions has been presented with little evidential base. The implication of these assertions is that part of the source of intergenerational poverty among blacks could be eliminated if illegitimate births could be prevented.

The conception of children out of wedlock is often described as a way of life for low-income women, a cultural norm. William Goode believes that many low-income women have few attributes other than sex at their disposal in the process of bargaining for husbands. He arrives at this conclusion based on his study of illegitmancy in the Caribbean Islands (Goode 1960: 20-30). It should go without saying that lower-class women often are exploited by men who have no intention of marrying. But the fact remains that the illegitimate child is sometimes a by-product of the woman's search for a husband. In these cases, the woman misunderstands the paramour and miscalculates, with tragic results.

THE CULTURE OF THE POOR

In general, persons who hypothesize that poverty is intergenerationally transmitted because of deficiencies in the person, family, and clan believe that there is a "culture of the poor" (Lewis 1962: 2). This concept, which may help organize our thoughts about the poor, also may tend to inhibit our perceptions of the great variations in behavior among poor people. A range of behavior patterns exists among poor people just as a range of behavior pattern exists among the nonpoor. Thus, it is inappropriate to look upon the poor as constituting a subculture that reinforces and perpetuates itself, including the condition of poverty. Our studies, which revealed diversified behavior in rent payment practices and in family activities among households in a low-rent public housing project in Syracuse, New York, cast doubt upon the concept of a culture of the poor

(Willie, Wagenfeld, and Cary 1964: 465-470). Of course, there are deficiencies in the life-style of some poor people as there are deficiencies in the life-style of others in the society. But these deficiencies should not be interpreted as an internally consistent, normative, and integrated pattern or a system of beliefs that guide and give direction to behavior that perpetuates poverty.

POVERTY AND THE SOCIAL SYSTEM

A hypothesis in opposition to the one discussed above is not formulated to explain whether or not poverty is transmitted intergenerationally. However, it does focus upon deficiencies in social systems and in the community at large. This alternative hypothesis is that change in social organization tends to be associated with change in individual behavior. According to this hypothesis, povety is a function of inadequacies in the operations of social systems; thus. systemic changes are necessary to eliminate poverty among individuals. By implication, then, this hypothesis is relevant to the debate about intergenerational transmissions of poverty. The background for this hypothesis is what has happened in this nation, as well as what is known to date about the intergenerational transmission of poverty.

The significant reduction in the proportion of low-income families during the past three decades has occurred largely because of change in the economic system. This system has continued to grow and expand, increasing in productivity and efficiency, and has brought more income to people through the years. Thus, much of the poverty that might have been perpetuated intergenerationally was eliminated as a consequence of systemic change — the growth and expansion of the economy.

Certain specific studies of intergenerational poverty also cast doubt on its transmission through families. One, for example, conducted by Lawrence Podell in New York City, discovered that only "15 per cent of a citywide sampling of mothers on welfare rolls ... had parents who also had been relief recipients." Moreover, Podell found that "eight out of ten believed their children would not become dependent adults."In the light of the experience of the mothers included in this study, there is reason to believe that their predictions might be realized; less than 2 out of 10 of current recipients came from families that received welfare assistance (*New York Times* 1968). (Failure to receive welfare, however, does not indicate automatically that 85 percent of the mothers came from non-poor families. In spite of public concern about increasing welfare rolls, it is a well-known fact that a large majority of poor families do not receive needed assistance.) Limiting the analysis to welfare families, however, one finds little evidence to support the contention that poverty is transmitted intergenerationally. The evidence indicates that intergenerational transmission is experienced in only a few families.

EDUCATION: Pro and Con

Many analysts who subscribe to the system change hypothesis as a more fruitful approach to an adequate explanation of poverty believe that the best way to eliminate it is to move in on the educational system. For instance, a report issued by the Upjohn Institute for Employment Research stated that "the keystone of any attempt to broaden the employment possibilities for blacks is obviously education — not only the formal programs of kindergarten through high school but also education that is now available in the form of training programs financed by various federal agencies" (Sheppard and Striner 1966: 22). However, psychiatrists Abram Kardiner and Lionel Ovesey have not held much hope for manipulation of the educational system as a way of dealing with poverty, especially among blacks, unless there is also a corresponding change in the education of white people. They state that "the psychosocial expressions of the black personality are the ... end products of the process of oppression. They can never be eradicated without removing the forces that create and perpetuate them. What is needed by the black is not education but re-integration. It is the white ... who requires the education . ... There is only one way that the products of oppression can be dissolved," according to Kardiner and Ovesey, "and that is to stop the oppression" (Kardiner and Ovesey 1962: 387). These two psychiatrists consider the inadequate education of blacks — and whatever association may exist between their poverty and education — to be the result of antiblack prejudice and discrimination.

Robert Merton, in his essay "The Self-Fulfilling Prophecy," supports this view in an illustration of the mechanism at work: "Whites who prophesy that blacks are incompetent and incapable of benefiting from formal education withhold support from black schools [making them inferior] and then point to the smaller number of black high school or college graduates [which the inferior schools produce] as justification for not providing greater support for the education of blacks" (Merton 1949: 179-195). In his commentary on schools in metropolitan areas, James B. Conant observed that "we now recognize so plainly but so belatedly [that] a caste system finds its clearest manifestation in an educational system" (Conant 1961: 11-12).

If the educational system in this country is to change so that it serves the needs of black people better, those people who established and continue to maintain a system of inferior education for blacks must change. They must support an educational system that equips blacks with the skills to participate productively in the mainstream of a technology-dominated economy. This, however, is not likely to occur unless whites are reoriented in their education and general socialization to relate to blacks as human beings, divested of any belief that whites are superhuman. Kardiner and Ovesey (1962: 379) point out that blacks were subjected to pure utilitarian use during the period of slavery in this country. "Once you degrade someone in that way," they remind us, "the sense of guilt makes it imperative to degrade the object further to justify the entire procedure." Merton doubts the efficacy of education as a way of dealing with the prevailing patterns of race relations. His belief is that "education may serve as an operational adjunct but not as the chief basis for any but excruciating slow change in the prevailing patterns of race relations." What is likely to be more effective, according to Merton, is "deliberate institutional change" designed to destroy discrimination (Merton 1949: 183, 193).

RACIAL DISCRIMINATION AND POVERTY

Economist Herman Miller, who also subscribes to the hypothesis of institutional change as a way of dealing with poverty among disadvantaged minority groups, maintains that "racial discrimination is a key cause" of the black's perpetually low estate. He refers to a study of the Council of Economic Advisers that estimated that during a single year billions of dollars more than they received would have been placed in the hands of blacks had there not been any racial discrimination in employment (Miller 1965:32). He points out that black people with the same amount of education as whites usually earn less money. In an analysis of the Census, Miller discovered that "non-white men earn about three-fourths as much as whites with the same amount of schooling," and that "blacks who have completed four years of college education can expect to earn only as much in a lifetime as whites who have not gone beyond the eighth grade." Thus, Miller concludes, "there is some justification for the feeling by Puerto Ricans, blacks, and other minority groups that education does not do as much for them, financially, as it does for others" (Miller 1964: 140-153).

It would appear that racial and ethnic discrimination more than inadequate education is one of the chief factors contributing to the low-income status of many blacks. For example, among whites of limited education (with eight or fewer years of schooling), 50 percent are likely to have jobs as service workers or laborers at the bottom of the heap, while nearly 80 percent of black workers with limited education are likely to find work only in these kinds of jobs (Miller 1964: 140-153).

James Tobin has pointed out that the low earning capacity of blacks and their inferior education "both reflect discrimination" (Tobin 1965: 878-898). The point I continue to emphasize, however, is that even when work capacity and education are equal of those of whites, discrimination still persists and results in a lower family income for blacks. The Moynihan thesis that the lack of improvement in opportunities for a large mass of black workers is correlated with a serious weakening of the black family, therefore, obscures the issue of discrimination and white racism in the United States, and so does his statement that "equality, as a fundamental democratic disposition, goes beyond equal opportunity to the issue of equal results" (Moynihan 1965: 746-747). The Census data analyzed by Miller indicated that equal opportunity has not yet been realized for black Americans; thus discussion of equal results is indeed premature.

We know that the rise in income in the past 20 to 30 years has been shared by black and by white families, and that the percentages of black and of white families below the poverty line have been significantly reduced, according to the U.S. Bureau of Labor Statistics (1967:18). The two populations, however, started from different bases. Of black families, 65 percent were poor two to three decades ago, compared with only 27 percent of white families. The proportion of blacks in poverty was two to three times greater than the proportion of poor whites two to three decades ago, and this ratio has remained constant over the years, even though the number of poor families has been reduced in each racial population (1967:18).

DIFFERENT APPROACHES FOR ELIMINATING POVERTY AMONG WHITES AND AMONG BLACKS

Because there are more than twice as many poor blacks proportionately as there are poor whites, and because racial discrimination has been identified as a key cause that keeps blacks at the bottom (an experience that they do not share with poor whites), it could very well be that different hypotheses are needed for explaining the continuation of poverty in the two racial populations. Failure to explore the possibility that different explanations of poverty may be required for different racial populations, which have had essentially different experiences, may have contributed to the contemporary controversy. It is conceivable, for example, that the hypothesis that may contribute to a better understanding of poverty among whites is one that seeks to determine the association, if any, among low-income status, motivation, aspiration, and life orientation. For blacks, however, a more powerful explanation of poverty might proceed from an examination of the hypothesis that seeks to determine the association, if any, among low-income status, racial discrimination, and institutional oppression.

The findings of another study that I conducted in Washington, D.C. are the basis for suggesting the possibility of differential explanations of poverty in white and in black populations. The study dealt with juvenile delinquency among whites and among blacks. I discovered that reducing family instability would probably contribute to a greater reduction in delinquency among whites than among blacks, and that increasing economic opportunities would very likely contribute to a greater reduction in delinquency among blacks than among whites. While a good deal of family instability existed with the black population in Washington, economic insecurity was overwhelming. It appeared, according to the data collected, that we could not get at the family instability factor and its association with delinquency without first dealing with economic insecurity and its association with delinquency. Because a higher proportion of whites were not poor, family instability was their outstanding problem. But economic insecurity was the salient problem for blacks, and it could not be circumvented in favor of family instability (Willie 1967).

The same principle may apply to the issue of poverty. Institutional changes during the past three to four decades have resulted in a substantial reduction in the proportion of whites who are poor. External changes in social organizations have upgraded most of the white population beyond the poverty level. The few who remain poor probably have problems that are more personal and less susceptible to mass amelioration through institutional manipulation. These whites may be the individuals with insufficient motivation, low aspiration, and a fatalistic orientation unreached thus far by changes in the institutional systems of society that create new opportunities. The proportion of poor blacks, however, remains at a higher level and may still be amenable to ameliorative mass efforts. Apparently, the kinds of institutional changes needed to upgrade the black population are somewhat different from those required to upgrade the white population. In addition to deliberate institutional changes that may increase economic opportunities, blacks require deliberate institutional changes that will prevent racial discrimination. Until these are put into effect, we cannot know how large the residual proportion of black poor people might be who need such individualized attention as the few poor whites may now require. To date, two-thirds of the black population have been upgraded beyond poverty. There is every reason to believe that more can and must be done.

A PROBLEM WITH THE MOYNIHAN PROPOSAL

In the light of this discussion, it would seem that one problem with the Moynihan proposal for dealing with poverty is that it projects a solution more appropriate for the white than for the black poor. One essential difference between blacks and whites with reference to poverty is that blacks also experience a great deal of discrimination and that the institutional changes that helped pull more than 9 out of every 10 whites above the poverty line have not run their full course for blacks. That is why the Moynihan concern about equal results is premature until there are equal opportunities.

CONCLUSIONS

On the basis of the foregoing analysis, we may derive the following conclusions:
1. There is some intergenerational transmission of poverty, though not as much as is generally assumed.
2. Upward social mobility is a more common experience in the United States than the continuation of intergenerational poverty.

3. The perpetuation of poverty from one generation to the next is likely to be a function of personal and family-connected circumstances as well as of patterns of institutional organization.
4. Personal and family-connected circumstances are likely to be more powerful explanations of poverty among whites than among blacks.
5. Institutional arrangements and patterns of racial discrimination are likely to be more powerful explanations of poverty among blacks than among whites.

The latter two conclusions are stated tentatively and should be further tested as hypotheses. The reason for suggesting a differential explanation for the continuation of poverty by race is the fact that whites and blacks have dissimilar patterns of participation in the economic system of the United States. As stated by Louis Kriesberg (1968: 5-6), "generational change in the proportion of the population which is poor is largely determined by economic developments and public policies regarding income maintenance and distribution." Racial discrimination has prevented blacks and other nonwhite minorities from participating fully in the benefits of an expanding economy. Changes in institutional arrangements have been largely responsible for preventing poverty among whites, and there is reason to believe that such changes will aid in the prevention of poverty among blacks if the benefits of these changes are made available to all sectors of society.

Because whites, in general, have had free access to the opportunities produced by institutional change, the residual number of poor people in this racial category might well be a function of personal and family-connected deficiencies. It is not concluded that poverty among whites cannot be further reduced by more changes in the institutional systems of society. Rather, it is suggested that new manipulations of social institutions will probably net a smaller rate of change in the proportion of poor whites as compared with poor blacks, for most whites who could benefit from these major institutional changes probably have already taken advantage of them.

REFERENCES

Conant, James B. 1961. *Slums and Suburbs.* New York: McGraw-Hill.

Glazer, Nathan, and Daniel Patrick Moynihan. 1964. *Beyond the Melting Pot.* Cambridge, MA: M.I.T. Press and Harvard University Press.

Goode, William J. 1960. "Illegitimacy in the Caribbean Social Structure." *American Sociological Review* 25 (February): 20-30.

Kardiner, Abram, and Lionel Ovesey. 1962. *The Mark of Oppression.* Cleveland: Meridian Books.

Kriesberg, Louis. 1968. "Intergenerational Patterns of Poverty." Paper presented at the annual meeting of the Eastern Sociological Society, Boston, April 6.

Lewis, Oscar. 1962. *Five Families.* New York: Science Editions.

Merton, Robert K. 1949. *Social Structure and Social Theory.* New York: Free Press.

Miller, Herman. 1965. "The Dimensions of Poverty." In *Poverty as a Public Issue,* edited by Ben E. Seligman. New York: Free Press.

_____. 1964. *Rich Man, Poor Man.* New York: Thomas Y. Crowell.

Morgan, N., et al. 1962. *Income and Welfare in the United States.* New York: McGraw-Hill

Moynihan, Daniel Patrick. 1965. "Employment, Income, and the Ordeal of the Negro Family." *Daedalus* 94 (Fall): 745-770.

New York Times. 1968. "Survey of Relief Shows Tie to Past." March 24.

Orshansky, Mollie. 1965. "Consumption, Work, and Poverty." In *Poverty as a Public Issue,* edited by Ben E. Seligman. New York: Free Press.

Sheppard, Harold L., and Herbert E. Striner. 1966. *Civil Rights, Employment, and the Social Status of American Negroes.* Kalamazoo: W.E. Upjohn Institute for Employment Research.

Tobin, James. 1965. "On Improving the Economic Status of the Negro." *Daedalus* 94 (Fall): 878-898.

U.S. Bureau of Labor Statistics. 1967. Bureau of Labor Statistics and Bureau of the Census, *Social and Economic Conditions of Negroes in the United States.* BLS Report no. 332, Current Population Reports, Series P-23, no. 24. Washington, D.C.: Government Printing Office.

U.S. Department of Labor. 1965. *The Negro Family. A Case for National Action.* Washington, D.C.: Government Printing Office.

Willie, Charles V. 1967. "Family Status and Economic Status in Juvenile Delinquency." *Social Problems* 14 (Winter): 326-335.

_____. 1960. "Age, Status, and Residential Stratification." *American Sociological Review* (April).

_____, Morton O. Wagenfeld, and Lee J. Cary. 1964. "Patterns of Rent Payment Among Problem Families." *Social Casework* 45 (October): 465-470.

PART IV

CONCLUSION

Chapter **11** A THEORETICAL
EXPLANATION OF
FAMILY ADAPTATION
BY RACE AND BY
SOCIAL CLASS

I have tried to describe the ways of life characteristic of
black families in different social classes. In many respects this
analysis is a continuation of that set in motion years ago by E.
Franklin Frazier, who hypothesized that "the social stratification of community ... would provide the most important frame
of reference for studying the social changes in the life of [blacks]
or any other urbanized group" (Frazier 1968: 141). Stratification among black families was largely ignored by other social
scientists in the past mainly because of the small number of affluent blacks and also because of the tendency to stereotype
blacks. By his own reckoning in an article published near the
mid-point of the twentieth century, Frazier stated that only
about one-eighth of the black families in the South, where most
black families resided at that time, were able to maintain a
middle-class way of life (Frazier 1968:207). These families,
small in number but influential, would have remained invisible
had it not been for Frazier's research and publication.

The final trimester of the twentieth century presents a different set of circumstances. No longer may anyone say, "a black
family is a black family is a black family." Differentiation
among blacks is a fact of life that should be described, explained,
and understood. As mentioned in Chapter 1, about 1 out of
every 3 black families has an annual income at or above the national median. This affluent population of racial minority
families is balanced by an indigent or poor category of about
one-third. Notwithstanding the gains in affluent status, black

208

families in the United States still must exist on a median annual income that is 30 to 40 percent less than that for whites. Clearly, differentiation in economic resources exists between the races and among blacks. The analysis in this book has demonstrated that these variations are associated with differing styles of living. This finding is related to another issue discussed by Frazier. His friend and colleague, G. Franklin Edwards, tells us that Frazier maintained a lively controversy with anthropologist Melville Herskovits about Herskovits's claim that "the [black] family continued to be influenced by African survivals;" Frazier disagreed and insisted that "the [black] family was a peculiar expression of response to the American environment" (Edwards 1968:xvi).

Frazier's belief that blacks had assimilated the cultural ways of the United States placed him squarely in the social theory camp of functional structuralism. According to Walter Wallace, such theorists "define the social in terms of objective behavior relations and seek to explain it by referring to phenomena that are socially generated through characteristics of the participants' environments." In other words, that which is social is a consequence of the behavior of one group toward others (Wallace 1969:161).

Thus, the way of life of black families and differentiation in life-styles among these families can be understood best by examining the macroenvironmental setting within which they live and the groups with which they interact, rather than by referring back to Africa or to the historical United States and the institution of slavery. Studies of family stability and income support Frazier's situational analysis. For example, in most affluent households there is no difference by race in the proportion of one-parent families; 5 percent of the white families compared to 6 percent of the black families are headed by women in the highest income category (U.S. Census 1969). Delinquent behavior among juveniles also is situationally determined. A Washington, D.C. study reveals that the lowest rate for black and for white populations is found in the same kinds of neighborhoods — those that are characterized by higher income and few broken families (Willie 1970:265).

The fact, however, that black families and white families exhibit similar overt responses to similar situations does not suggest that there are no differences in adaptations by race. Indeed, the subjective responses of whites and of blacks to similar situations may be quite different, because of their dominant and subdominant positions in the community power structure as majority and minority populations. The effort required of blacks compared to whites to reach the same level of achievement may be unequal, when racial discrimination is factored in. Moreover, a similar experience probably has different meanings for dominant and subdominant populations.

Frazier recognized the minority as a mirror of society and said that the study of blacks could lead to an understanding of the adaptations of other human beings. Particularly did he believe that study of the black family adjustments might lead to "a clearer understanding of the relation of human motivation to culture" (Frazier 1968:191). But Frasier never extracted from his studies of blacks propositions applicable to other population groups.

Frazier, in effect, abandoned his theoretical position of functional structuralism and the search for commonalities toward the close of his life, when he attempted to explain the consumer behavior of affluent blacks as a function of their alleged isolation from the American social system rather than as a function of the nature of their participation in it. In two of his more polemical essays, written in 1957 and in 1962, he described blacks and especially affluent blacks as "outsiders in American life" (Frazier 1968:270), who created "a world of make-believe" (Frazier 1968:255). But earlier, he claimed that "the [black] family had become largely oriented to the values of the American culture." He pointed toward their "conspicuous consumption" as an indicator of commitment to the values of Amercan culture" (Frazier 1968:207). E. Franklin Frazier, a leading black sociologist and former president of the American Sociological Association, died in 1962 and left unresolved this apparent contradiction — his assertion that affluent blacks were both committed to and isolated from the values of American culture. As a continuation of the study of Frazier, my goal is to resolve the contradiction, if possible.

I think that a structural-functionalist perspective is helpful in analyzing variations of life-styles of families in this society, including both black families and white families. I believe that the adaptations of the affluent are no less deviant than the adaptations of the poor or of the working class. As stated by Robert Nisbet, "all human behavior is normatively directed." Nisbet continues, "It is impossible for human beings to be in continuous association and interaction with one another for long without a culture arising ... norms are the vital core of culture." He describes norms as the ends and purposes in life that are, so to speak, waiting for us in the social order when we are born (Nisbet 1970:222-224). Ends might be translated as goals. Robert Merton believes that some goals in society transcend class lines (Merton 1949:137,133). In view of the extended interaction between black and white populations for several centuries in the United States and also the close association between black families of different social classes in black ghettos of the United States, some goals in common must have developed. For this reason the means-ends schema developed by Merton in his essay "Social Structure and Anomie" appears to be an appropriate vehicle for explaining adaptations of families by race and social class. In Table 1, (+) signifies "acceptance," (−) signifies "rejection," and (±) signifies "rejection of prevailing values and substitution of new values." In brackets is the innovative adaptation Type III that Merton classifies as ritualism, which seems to me to be an alternative to his Type II. The ritualization definition by Merton was contaminated by social class concepts. Innovation as used here can appear in any social class and refers to either goals or means.

Merton identifies five kinds of adaptations by individuals to social organization: conformity, innovation, ritualism, retreatism, rebellion. This typology is a conceptual approach to an understanding of the differences in adaptations among affluent, working-class, and poor families.

Merton recognized the value of situational analysis by calling our attention to the fact "that people may shift from one alternative [adaptation] to another as they engage in different spheres of social activities." Thus, he said the categories in the typology "refer to role behavior in specific types of situations, not to personality" (Merton 1949:133). The adaptations by race and social class then are situationally, not biologically, determined. The situation of blacks in American society, for example, is that of a minority or subdominant population in the power structure that receives an inequitable amount of the nation's wealth. The survival requirements for dominant and subdominant populations differ, and so do those for affluent and poor families. Compassion is a fundamental form of behavior that dominants must exhibit in their interaction with subdominants to prevent rebellion against the existing social order. Courage and endurance are essential among subdominants who would resist and overcome the oppression of dominants. The behavior requirements of groups differ depending on their situation in the social system, their goals, and the methods available to them.

Table 1
A TYPOLOGY OF MODES OF
INDIVIDUAL ADAPTATION
(From Merton 1949:133)

Modes of Adaptation	Cultural Goals	Institutionalized Means
I. Conformity	+	+
II. Innovation	+	−
III. [Innovation]*	−	+
IV. Retreatism	−	−
V. Rebellion	±	±

*Identified as Ritualism in the original table.

Merton states that stability results from adaptation Type I — conformity to both cultural goals and institutionalized means (Merton 1949:134). This is precisely the adaptation that is manifested by affluent blacks. Far from being isolated from

American cultural values, as Frazier claimed, affluent blacks are central in the maintenance of such values. Former Transportation Secretary William Coleman once said that whites owe a debt of gratitude to blacks for making the U.S. Constitution work (Willie 1978). It is interesting to note that the most famous black lawyers are constitutional experts. Richard Kluger said that Thurgood Marshall's "record of success as a civil-rights lawyer had begun to turn him into a legend" (Kluger 1975:18).

The affluent black families analyzed in Part II of this study are conformists to both the cultural goals of this nation and the prescribed means for fulfilling these goals. Their values reflect the philosophy of Thomas Jefferson, one of the founders of this nation, who believed that education should be available to all so that the citizens in a democracy could make moral decisions about governance for the common good; that ability rather than wealth or family connection should be the basis for community leadership; and that democratic decision-making by the people is a virtuous and wise way of arriving at just solutions. The values of affluent black families reflect the U.S. Constitution, the legal norm of our society, and its requirement of equal protection of the laws for all.

Affluent white families, on the other hand, subscribe to democracy as a method of social organization but not fully to its goals. They adapt acording to Merton's Type III. They are innovationists in that they seek to change the goals as a way of frustrating those who might lay claim to their privileged position, but they insist that all use agreed-upon means to achieve power and authority in society, although such means may not be available to or suitable for subdominant people in the power structure who do not have a head start. Because affluent white families are anxious sometimes that others may invade their territory or turf they, in colloquial terminology, try to change the name of the game as a way of eliminating challengers, and they contend that such is fair in a free enterprise system.

H. R. Mencken is an example of an affluent white individual who believed in the method of democracy so much that he attended national political conventions as a news analyst and wrote a book on *Making a President*. Yet, he published a "Proposed New Constitution for Maryland" that, among other undemocratic goals, "advocated creating a grand inquest — a group of outstanding citizens to monitor the conduct of government." A Virginia Law School professor dubbed Mencken's proposed constitution "an honest effort to combine personal liberty and fascism" (Moss 1980:162). Freedom is a method of social organization; fascism or fraternity are goals. Many white affluent individuals believe in the democratic method but think that society and its institutions should be controlled by an intellectual elite. Those who subscribe to this approach are called innovationists because such a way differs from the vision of American society contained in the Declaration of Independence and the Constitution, our normative documents.

White working-class families appear to be content to settle for a modest place in life. Both mothers and fathers tend to work, usually in clerical or semiskilled jobs, or in service work. The father or husband in the household sometimes looks upon himself as a failure, although he may be a steady worker. Thus, the parents tend to invest their dreams in their children's future. This is especially true of the mother or grandmother in the household, who is a chief source of emotional support for the children as well as the husband.

There is not much planning for the future in white working-class families. Everything seems to be oriented toward the present. The good life is having a good day, having a steady job, earning enough money to furnish a home and maybe own it, buy tools for a workshop, have a beer from time to time.

Working-class whites do not blame others for their fate. They tend to see themselves as inadequate for the requirements and responsibilities of their time. For this reason they tend not to have a dream of the kind of life they wish for themselves. They more or less drift, enjoying themselves when possible, conforming to the requirements of the situation in which they find themselves, doing what comes naturally, taking little initiative to change things.

Illness and death in white working-class families are nerve-wracking, unsettling experiences. They represent lost opportunities and unfair sentences of fate. They sometimes bring family members together, but they also are the source of escape behavior such as excess drinking and even physical abuse of one's spouse that drive families apart (Levinson 1978:126-135).

The young who grow up in such households experience a double bind: they are urged to love their parents but not to emulate them. The parents want a better future for their offspring, yet are fearful that their upwardly mobile children may disown them; they are hesitant to urge their offspring to strive for success. The children sometimes are resentful of their misfortune and the desire that parents have to perpetuate family culture and traditions. Education is the social mobility elevator that the children in the white working class sometimes board for movement away from their working-class roots and origin. Education for a few is seen as a great escape (Lewis 1979: 36-37).

The children may complain, but seldom do their parents. The work of the parents may be unrewarding, but they endure. They may have low self-esteem, but they do not despair. They know how to sacrifice, and they do it willingly, especially for their children. They declare that the world does not owe them a living. If a woman has a man who loves to work, she considers herself lucky, never mind the kind of work her husband does. The white working class pledges allegiance to the flag and tends to accept society as it is. The white working-class family knows of hard times. Its members endure hard work, and do not ask for help from anyone. This is how the white working-class family survives, when it does survive. During periods of economic stress, family disintegration increases.

Like the affluent black family, the working-class black family is conformist, and adapts according to Type I — upholding cultural goals and following institutionalized means, believing in self-reliance, accepting the free enterprise system and its opportunities for success or failure. Of their circumstances, they blame themselves and not the system. They pledge allegiance to the goals and methods of American society, although the system seems to have left them behind (Wrobel 1976).

Black working-class families are also innovationists, but their adaptation is different from that of affluent whites, who believe in the institutionalized means but who reject the cultural goal of equal opportunity for all in an open society. The black working class is innovative because its members accept the cultural goals but reject the means for their achievement, largely because these means are unavailable. For the black working class, the opportunity system may be blocked. Its members experience a closed, not an open, society, and must improvise to make their way through. Their adaptation is according to Type II. They strive to achieve, by any means.

The poor are as much a part of society as the members of families in any other social class position. The mainstream values of American culture are well understood by them. Charles Valentine (1971:103) said that these values receive general allegiance among blacks. Among poor whites, mainstream values are undertsood too, so much so, that these families are reluctant to relate to others of a higher status who, they believe, might try to make them feel ashamed of their lot in life (Wilkes 1977:99). Even though the white poor know that there is a better life, they tend to limit what they permit themselves to wish for as one way of "making life tolerable" and less frustrating (Knupfer 1953:263). In general, Sally Bould-Vantil found that "the attitudes of the poor ... do not differ from the non-poor in terms of their aspirations in the world of work" (Bould-Vantil 1976:151).

Poor blacks tend to live in urban ghettoes; poor whites may not. Poor blacks appear to have a community support system of kin and friends; poor whites do not — they usually have only their relatives to rely upon. Poor whites are proud, and accept their circumstances as a function of fate. Poor blacks are resentful and rage at a discriminating society thay they believe has treated them unfairly. Being only one-tenth of the majority population, poor whites are more or less invisible and all but forgotten by others of their race. Being at least one-third of the population of the minority, poor blacks are a sufficient critical mass to demand consideration of their concerns in any social action agenda. Under these circumstances and conditions, one might expect a different pattern of adaptation to social organization by the black and the white poor.

In general, poor whites adapt in a retreating fashion, according to Merton's Type IV. They tend to give up on any hope of ever fulfilling culturally prescribed goals through legitimate institutional means. One might call such families the socially disinherited who have assimilated the goals, rules, and regulations of society but who have found all avenues to them inaccessible. Merton describes their mode of adaptation as that of frustrated and handicapped individuals who cannot cope and who, therefore, drop out. They experience defeatism and resignation, manifested in escape mechanisms such as drinking, gambling, and fighting. It is important to recognize that the retreatism is a way of reducing conflict that arises from internalization of the legitimate goals and means for achievement and the inability to use the illegitimate route because of internalized prohibitions (Merton 1949:142-143).

There are few structural supports for poor white families, who tend to be isolated from others in rural areas or as invisible residents of the inner city. They are members of few organizaitons. Family members work when work is available; but the kinds of jobs that they can hold are neither plentiful nor stable. Thus the women in the household in service occupations are sometimes more regularly employed than are their menfolk. The families tend to be stoic and take whatever comes in stride. They do not like to receive charity and boast of the fact that they are not on welfare.

These poor white families are children-centered. Usually, they are large. Once could call children the treasure of poor whites. They enjoy seeing them develop the spirit of survival, which includes being tough. Such families have their share of tragedies. One or more members may be victims of homocide; divorce and desertion are frequent; getting into trouble with law enforcement authorities is commonplace; medical problems go unattended and sometimes result in unnecessary deaths.

For these poor white individuals, their family is their world. Others tend to shun them. The mother is the hub of the family. Everything tends to revolve around her. She is the person of wisdom; she is the undisputed authority. She is the person who perseveres, caring for the sick, getting members out of jail, and working when she can. Despite her heroic efforts, nothing seems to be effective. Thus, the poor white family is submissive, tends to withdraw, lacks self-confidence, limits its participation in social organization, and tends to be fatalistic (Knupfer 1953; Wilkes 1977; Bould-Vantil 1976).

The poor black family is rebellious. Their adaptation is Merton's Type V. They press for a modified social structure that will accommodate their concerns and grant them some measure of consideration. They want a society in which there is a "closer correspondence between ... effort and reward" (Merton 1949:145). Seeing that the existing society is organized against them, the black poor veto "business as usual." They do not accept their position as a condition of fate. When they no longer can endure, they riot and rebel, hoping to draw attention to their circumstances, hoping that others will then set things right. Through their rebellion, poor blacks attempt "to change the existing cultural and social structure rather than to accommodate efforts within the structure" (Merton 1949:379). Merton reminds us, however, that the renegade who "renounces the prevailing values ... becomes the target of greatest hostility ... " (Merton 1949:146). This has been the lot of poor black families. The society has resented and raged against them as much as they have resented and raged against society (Geismar 1973; Jeffers 1970; Shulz 1970).

The neat way in which the life-styles by race and social class fit into the theoretical schema developed by Merton for explaining variation in adaptations to social organization suggests that all American families — including affluent, working-class, and poor black and white families — participate in and share a common core of values. Black families are not isolated from the values of American society as Frazier once claimed. Martin Luther King, Jr. contended that blacks were concerned with fulfilling the American Dream. Schematically, the way that black and white families adapt to Amercian society is shown in Table 2.

On the basis of this analysis we may conclude (1) that black

Table 2

A TYPOLOGY OF MODES OF ADAPTATION
IN AMERICAN SOCIETY BY RACE AND SOCIAL CLASS

Social Class	Black Families		White Families	
	Mode of Adaptation		Mode of Adaptation	
	Cultural Goals	Institutional Means	Cultural Goals	Institutional Means
Affluent	+	+	−	+
Working class	+	−	+	+
Poor	±	±	=	=

Note: + Conformity to goals and means

− Nonconformity to goals and means

± Resistance to goals and means in an aggressive, rebellious way

= Resistance to goals and means in a passive, retreating way

families and white families in the United States share a common core of values, (2) that they adapt to the society and its values in different ways, largely because of their dominant and subdominant situations, and (3) that the unique adaptations of racial populations are further differentiated by variations in style of life by social class. Thus, any assumption that the life of blacks in the United States can be understood independently of their involvement with whites appears to be unwarranted. The same may be said of the way of life of whites. Moreover, the life-style of one social class cannot be understood apart from that of other social classes.

Referring to the interdependence of individuals, races, and social classes in the United States, I am reminded of the wisdom of George Bernard Shaw's character Eliza Doolittle, who said that she discovered that the difference between a flower girl and a lady is not so much how she acts but how she is treated. My modified version of her statement is that the difference between individuals, social classes, and races in society is how they act as well as how they are treated. We know this because we have analyzed the intimate details of black family life, using a unique approach of combining data obtained from case interviews with survey research. These two methods enabled us to understand the habits of individuals, the customs of families, the life-styles of social classes, and the adaptations of a race from the point of view of the people studied and also in terms of a logical schema of social theory. The purpose of this book has been to place the discussion of race and social class differentiation among black families in the United States within a theoretical framework.

Further research is needed to compare the rich detail derived from an analysis of case studies of black families by social class with an analysis of case studies of white families by social class.

REFERENCES

Anthropology Today. 1971. Del Mar, CA: CRM Books.
Bould-Vantil, Sally. 1976. *Work and the Culture of Poverty.* San Fran-

cisco: R and E Research Associates.

Edwards, G. Franklin. 1968. "Introduction." In *Franklin Frazier on Race Relations,* edited by G. Franklin Edwards. Chicago: University of Chicago Press.

Frazier, E. Franklin. 1968. "The Failure of the Negro Intellectual," "The Negro Family in America," and "Inferiority Complex and Quest for Status." In *Franklin Frazier on Race Relations,* edited by G. Franklin Edwards. Chicago: University of Chicago Press.

Geismar, Ludwig. 1973. *555 Families.* New Brunswick, NJ: Transaction Books.

Jeffers, Camille. 1970. "Mother and Children in Public Housing." In *The Family Life of Black People,* edited by Charles V. Willie. Columbus: Charles E. Merrill.

Kluger, Richard. 1975. *Simple Justice.* New York: Vintage Books.

Knupfer, Genevieve. 1953. "Portrait of the Underdog." In *Class, Status, and Power,* edited by Reinhard Bendix and Seymour Martin Lipset. New York: Free Press.

Levinson, Daniel J. 1978. *The Seasons of a Man's Life.* New York: Ballantine.

Lewis, James. 1979. "The Melting Pot Myth." *Syracuse University Alumni News* 59 (Summer).

Merton, Robert K. 1949. *Social Structure and Social Theory.* New York: Free Press.

Moss, Malcolm. 1980. "Mencken, Politics, and Politicians." In *On Mencken,* edited by John Dorsey. New York: Alfred A. Knopf.

Nisbet, Robert A. 1970. *The Social Bond.* New York: Alfred A. Knopf.

Schulz, David. 1970. "The Role of the Boyfriend in Lower Class Negro Life." In *The Family Life of Black People,* edited by C.V. Willie, Columbus: Charles E. Merrill.

U.S. Census Bureau. 1969. *Trends in Social and Economic Conditions in Metropolitan Areas,* Series P-23, no. 27. Washington, D.C.: U.S. Government Printing Office.

Valentine, Bettylou. 1978. *Hustling and Other Hard Work.* New York: Free Press.

Wallace, Walter L. (ed.). 1969. *Sociological Theory.* Chicago: Aldine.

Wilkes, Paul. 1977. *Six American Families.* New York: Seabury.

Willie, Charles V. 1970. "The Relative Contribution of Family Status and Economic Status to Juvenile Delinquency." In *The Family Life of Black People,* edited by C.V. Willie. Columbus: Charles E. Merrill.

————. 1978. *The Sociology of Education.* Lexington, MA: Lexington Books.

Wrobel, Paul. 1976. "Polish American Men: As Workers, As Husbands, and as Fathers." Paper presented at American Association for the Advancement of Science, Boston, February 18-24.

APPENDIX

INTERVIEW SCHEDULE
FOR PART II

An earlier form of this schedule was used for the study described in Chapter 9 in Part III.

#1
What is the name of the head of this household? Could you list the name of other persons who live here, including family, relatives, lodgers, if any? Write names in this order: Head of household on first line; spouse of head; unmarried children; oldest first, married children and their children; other relatives; lodgers

#2
What is the relationship of each person to the head of this household? (e.g., husband, wife, son, daughter, mother-in-law, etc.)

#3
What is the sex of each person? Write M for Male and F for Female

#4
Could you list the *year* in which the person was born?

#5
Could you list the race of each person?

Write in: Black, White, Other Race (list)

#6
Of what *nation* or country is this person a citizen?

Write in: U.S.A. Specify Other

Head of Household

1.
2.
3.
4.
5.
6.
7.
8.
9.
10.
11.
12.
13.

#7 With which cultural, ethnic, or nationality group do the members of this house identify? (e.g., Italian-American, Irish-American, German-American, specify others)	#8 What is the highest grade in school *completed* by this person? Write in: correct number and degree, if any. **ELEMENTARY Jr. Hi. Sr. Hi.** 1-2-3-4-5-6-7-8-9-10-11-12 **College** 1-2-3-4 **Graduate** 1-2-3-4-5 +	#9 What is the marital status of each person? Write in: married, separated, divorced, widowed, single	#10 How many years has this person been married, separated, divorced, or widowed? Write 0 for single people. Reference is to current status	#11 Has this person ever been married? If yes, write # of times YES NO
1.				
2.				
3.				
4.				
5.				
6.				
7.				
8.				
9.				
10.				
11.				
12.				
13.				

FOR EMPLOYED PERSONS ONLY

#12
Was this person *em-ployed* during this last week?

#13
Was this person looking for fulltime work during the past week?

#14
What is the *occupation* of this person? Write in job title or DK (Don't Know).

#15
What *work* does this person do? Write in description of job or DK (Don't Know). (If the kind of work that the person does indicates the job title, fill in the correct occupation for the previous question.)

A. Full Time   B. Part Time

YES	NO	YES	NO

	YES	NO

1.
2.
3.
4.
5.
6.
7.
8.
9.
10.
11.
12.
13.

FOR EMPLOYED PERSONS ONLY

#16 What *kind* of organization does this person work for?

a. Fed. Gov't
b. Local Gov't
c. Manufacturing
d. Construction
e. Transportation
f. Utilities
g. Private household (Domestic)
h. Wholesale store
i. Retail store
j. Real Estate
k. Insurance
l. Banking
m. Other (Specify)
n. DK (Don't Know)
o. Services (Specify)

#17 Is this the person's usual job?

YES

or

NO

#18 About how many days did each person spend in *bed* because of *illness* last year?

Write in number of days.

#19 In what *state* was this person born? If person was born outside U.S., in what country was he or she born?

Write in name or DK (Don't Know).

#20 How many *years* has this person lived in this city or metropolitan area?

1.
2.
3.
4.
5.
6.
7.
8.
9.
10.
11.
12.
13.

#21
In what state,
city or coun-
try did this
person live
before coming
to this city
or area?
(Write
"native" for
locally born.)

#22
What is the
religious
preference
of this
person?
Write in:
Denomina-
tion and
Protestant
Catholic
Jewish
None
other

#23
Does this person
attend a church
or synagogue?
write yes or no.

_____
YES   NO
_____
If yes,
how often?
____Week,
      Month

1._____
2._____
3._____
4._____
5._____
6._____
7._____
8._____
9._____
10._____
11._____
12._____
13._____

#24
Are there any offspring in this family who are not currently in this household? _____ YES _____ NO
If yes, could you tell me the age and sex of the offspring, whether or not they are still alive and in what city and state they live and how often you see them?

Name of Offspring Not at Home	Relation- ship to Head	Check: Male	Check: Fe- male	Check: Liv- ing	De- ceased	Year of Birth	Residence City	State	Don't Know	Daily	Weekly	Monthly	Visits Yr	Every 2Yr	5Yr	Never
1.																
2.																
3.																
4.																
5.																
6.																
7.																
8.																
9.																
10.																
11.																
12.																
13.																

#25
This question has to do with the offspring or dependent children in the household at this time.

Name of Child	Have any of the children listed ever been in trouble with the police or law enforcement authorities? If so, what was the problem and what was the outcome? Problem/Outcome	How would you describe the progress of each child in school: Does very well. Does about average work. Has trouble with teachers. Has learning disability. Has trouble with other students. Does not like school. Likes school.	How would you describe the adjustment of each child in the community: Has many playmates. Does not know other children. Gets along well with other children. Has fights and arguments often. Others pick on him or her.	Regarding discipline, how would you describe each child: Follows instructions well. Is rebellious. Looks out for other children. Is agreeable and pleasant. Is a discipline problem.	When this child needs to be disciplined, who does it? Write in mother, father, mother and father, grandmother, grandfather, aunt, uncle Other (Specify)
1.					
2.					
3.					
4.					
5.					
6.					
7.					
8.					
9.					
10.					
11.					
12.					
13.					

#25 (continued)

#26
This question has to do with the offspring who are adult and are no longer at home.

Name of Offspring	How old was this person when he or she left home?	Why did this person leave home? Write in: married, work, school, institution, other(specify)	How far in school did this person go? Did he or she receive a diploma or degree? If so, what was it?	What does this child plan to do when he or she is adult?	How much education will he or she need to hold this job?
1.					
2.					
3.					
4.					
5.					
6.					
7.					
8.					
9.					
10.					
11.					
12.					
13.					

#26 (continued)

What kind of work does this person do?	If offspring is married, what kind of work does spouse do?	When this person was growing up, did he or she ever get in trouble with the police or law enforcement agents?	How would you describe the progress of this person in school when growing up? Did very well. Did about average. Had learning disability. Had trouble with others. Did not like school. Liked school	How would you describe adjustment in community when this person was growing up? Had many playmates. Did not know others. Got along well. Had many fights. Others picked on him or her.	When this person needed discipline, who gave it? Write in: mother, father, mother and father, grandmother, grandfather, aunt, uncle, other (specify).
1.					
2.					
3.					
4.					
5.					
6.					
7.					
8.					
9.					
10.					
11.					
12.					
13.					

#27
If you were asked to classify your family, living in the household, would you say it is:

_____Real Close   _____Each person does his or her own thing   _____We don't do much together

_____Close   _____Everybody works together for a common goal

_____Not Close at All   _____We don't see much of each other

#28
Do you have a regular time for eating dinner or supper in your family?   _____Yes   _____No

#29
If the answer is yes, what hour of the day do you usually eat dinner?   _____PM

#30
Regarding daily family meals, which family members usually eat together? For instance, which family members usually eat breakfast, lunch and dinner together on a weekday like Monday through Friday? Which is typical of your family? What do you do on weekends?

#31
We are interested in what your family does on a weekend day, for instance, on Sunday, from 7:00 a.m. to midnight. Could you give an example of what each family member usually does?

7:00	8:00	9:00	10:00	11:00	12 Noon
1.					
2.					
3.					
4.					
5.					
6.					
7.					
8.					
9.					
10.					
11.					
12.					
13.					

1:00	2:00	3:00	4:00	5:00	6:00
1.					
2.					
3.					
4.					
5.					
6.					
7.					
8.					
9.					
10.					
11.					
12.					
13.					

7:00	8:00	9:00	10:00	11:00	12 Midnight
1.					
2.					
3.					
4.					
5.					
6.					
7.					
8.					
9.					
10.					
11.					
12.					
13.					

#32
We are interested in what your family does on a weekday, say, for instance, yesterday or the day before yesterday. From 7a.m. to midnight, could you tell us what each member of your family usually does? We could start with yourself.

7:00	8:00	9:00	10:00	11:00	12 Noon
1.					
2.					
3.					
4.					
5.					
6.					
7.					
8.					
9.					
10.					
11.					
12.					
13.					

1:00	2:00	3:00	4:00	5:00	6:00
1.					
2.					
3.					
4.					
5.					
6.					
7.					
8.					
9.					
10.					
11.					
12.					
13.					

7:00	8:00	9:00	10:00	11:00	12 Midnight
1.					
2.					
3.					
4.					
5.					
6.					
7.					
8.					
9.					
10.					
11.					
12.					
13.					

#33
We would like to get an estimate of your income. How much does your family receive (a week, a month, or a year). You may indicate the alphabet letter that is by the correct figure.

	Weekly		Monthly		Annual
a.	less than $80 (specify)	a.	less than $320	a.	less than $4160
b.	$ 80 to 99	b.	$ 320 to 399	b.	$ 4,160 to 5,199
c.	100 to 119	c.	400 to 479	c.	5,200 to 6,239
d.	120 to 139	d.	480 to 559	d.	6,240 to 7,279
e.	140 to 159	e.	560 to 639	e.	7,280 to 8,319
f.	160 to 179	f.	640 to 719	f.	8,320 to 9,359
g.	180 to 199	g.	720 to 799	g.	9,360 to 10,399
h.	200 to 219	h.	800 to 879	h.	10,400 to 11,439
i.	220 to 239	i.	880 to 959	i.	11,440 to 12,479
j.	240 to 259	j.	960 to 1039	j.	12,480 to 13,519
k.	260 to 279	k.	1040 to 1119	k.	13,520 to 14,559
l.	280 to 299	l.	1120 to 1199	l.	14,560 to 15,559
m.	300 to 319	m.	1200 to 1279	m.	15,600 to 16,639
n.	320 to 339	n.	1280 to 1359	n.	16,640 to 17,679
o.	340 to 359	o.	1360 to 1439	o.	17,680 to 18,719
p.	360 to 379	p.	1440 to 1519	p.	18,720 to 19,759
q.	380 to 399	q.	1520 to 1599	q.	19,760 to 20,799
r.	400 to 419	r.	1600 to 1679	r.	20,800 to 21,839
s.	420 to 439	s.	1680 to 1759	s.	21,840 to 22,879
t.	440 to 459	t.	1760 to 1839	t.	22,880 to 23,919
u.	460 to 479	u.	1840 to 1919	u.	23,920 to 24,959
v.	480 to 499	v.	1920 to 1999	v.	24,960 to 25,999
w.	500 to 519	w.	2000 to 2079	w.	26,000 to 27,039
x.	520 to 539	x.	2080 to 2159	x.	27,040 to 28,079
y.	540 to 559	y.	2160 to 2239	y.	28,080 to 29,119
z.	560 to 579	z.	2240 to 2319	z.	29,120 to 30,179
aa.	580 to 599	aa.	2320 to 2399	aa.	30,160 to 30,199
bb.	600 to 619	bb.	2400 to 2479	bb.	31,200 to 32,239
cc.	620 to 639	cc.	2480 to 2559	cc.	32,240 to 33,279
dd.	640 to 659	dd.	2560 to 2639	dd.	33,280 to 34,319
ee.	660 to 679	ee.	2640 to 2719	ee.	34,320 to 35,359
ff.	680 to 699	ff.	2720 to 2799	ff.	35,360 to 36,399
gg.	over 700 (give specific)	gg.	2800 and over	gg.	over 36,400

#34
How many wage earners are there in this household? _____
#35
What percent of the total family income comes from wages of each employed person in the household?

Wife_____
Husband_____
Children_____
Relatives_____
Friend_____
TOTAL   100%

COMMUNITY RELATIONS AND FOLKLORE

#36
Are you satisfied or dissatisfied with this neighborhood?

_____ Satisfied Completely
_____ Satisfied Somewhat
_____ Dissatisfied Somewhat
_____ Dissatisfied Completely

Why do you feel this way? _____

#37
Have you ever thought about moving away from this neighborhood? _____ Yes _____ No
Why do you want to move or stay? _____

If person wants to move: Where do you want to move? _____

#38
This neighborhood could be classified as a

_____ White neighborhood
_____ Black neighborhood
_____ Mixed neighborhood
_____ Other (write in)
_____ Don't know

#39
This neighborhood could be classified as a

_____ Working class
_____ Middle class
_____ Upper class
_____ Poor
_____ Don't know

#40
Most of the families in this neighborhood

_____ Have well-behaved children
_____ Have children that get into trouble
_____ Don't know

#41
In this neighborhood _____ the police do a fine job of enforcing the law
_____ the police are unfair
_____ the police do not care about enforcing the law
_____ Don't know

#42
Do you own or rent this dwelling unit? _____ own _____ rent
(If home is owned): About how much would you estimate this dwelling would sell for? $ _____
(If home is rented): What are the weekly $ _____ or monthly $ _____ payments?

#43
How many rooms are there in this dwelling unit used exclusively by this household?
_____ Kitchen _____ Bedroom _____ Living Room _____ Dining Room _____ Other (specify) _____ Total

#44
How would you describe this dwelling unit?
_____ a room _____ an apartment _____ a single-family home
_____ a flat _____ a duplex _____ Other (specify)

#45
Do you have a television? _____ Yes _____ No

#46
If yes, what kind of programs do you watch? _____

#47
About how long do you watch television each day? _____

#48
About how long do the children watch television each day? _____

#49
Do you have a radio _____ Yes _____ No

#50
Where do you hear about news? _____ TV _____ radio _____ paper _____ relatives or friends

#51
Do you get a daily paper? _____ Yes _____ No

#52
Do you get any other publications or magazines? _____ Yes _____ No
If yes, which? _____

#53
Do you have a telephone? _____ Yes _____ No

#54
What I like best about this neighborhood is _____

#55
What troubles me most about this neighborhood is _____

#56
About how many people in this neighborhood do you know? _____ Five to ten
_____ Ten to twenty
_____ Twenty to thirty
_____ Forty to fifty
_____ One to five
_____ None

#57
This neighborhood has a reputation as _____ a dangerous area
_____ a safe area
_____ in between safe and dangerous
_____ uncertain

#58
Why do you describe the neighborhood this way? _____

#59
If you had the power to change this neighborhood, what would you change? _____

#60
If you had the power to change this city, what would you change? _____

#61
Which person or persons would you turn to for help in an emergency or to deal with a problem you could not handle alone? If possible, tell us the name of the person you would turn to, what he or she does for a living, how this person is known by you, and why you would turn to him or her for help. _____

#62

We would like to get an understanding of how decisions are made in this household and who influences the decisions that are made. Could you please tell me who usually has the msot influence on some of the following decisions? (If there are no children in the household now, whom do you remember having the most influence when children were present?)

CHECK ONE THAT HAD MOST INFLUENCE

DECISION	Mother	Father	Mother Father Equal	Grand-mother	Grand-father	Other Specify	Does Not Apply or Don't Know
a. Helping children with homework							
b. Teaching children manners							
c. Taking care of sick children							
d. Deciding what to eat for meals							
e. Cooking							
f. Assigning chores to children in the home							
g. Helping children to decide how to spend money							
h. Going to school to talk with the teacher							
i. Deciding to move into this house							
j. Helping children to find part-time work							
k. Helping children to decide on adult occupations							
l. Deciding what job the head of the household should take							
m. Deciding on what political candidate to vote for							
n. Deciding what school to send children to							
o. Deciding on what church or synagogue to affiliate with							
p. Deciding on what political party to join							
q. Deciding on what car to buy							
r. Deciding on what furniture to buy							
s. Deciding on the number of children							

#63
What kinds of organizations, if any, does your spouse belong to?

A. Religious or Church Connected
1.
2.
3.
4.

E. Voluntary or Service
1.
2.
3.
4.

B. Lodge or Secret Society
1.
2.
3.
4.

F. Neighborhood Improvement
1.
2.
3.
4.

C. Recreational or Social
1.
2.
3.
4.

G. Social Action/Civil Rights
1.
2.
3.
4.

D. Political
1.
2.
3.
4.

H. Business, Professional or Work Ass'n
1.
2.
3.
4.

#64
What kinds of organizations, if any, do you belong to:

A. Religious or Church Connected
1.
2.
3.
4.

E. Voluntary or Service
1.
2.
3.
4.

B. Lodge or Secret Society
1.
2.
3.
4.

F. Neighborhood Improvement
1.
2.
3.
4.

C. Recreational or Social
1.
2.
3.
4.

G. Social Action/Civil Rights
1.
2.
3.
4.

D. Political
1.
2.
3.
4.

H. Business, Professional or Work Ass'n
1.
2.
3.
4.

#65
What kinds of organizations, if any, do the children in this household belong?

A. Religious or Church Connected
1.
2.
3.
4.

E. Voluntary or Service
1.
2.
3.
4.

B. Lodge or Secret Society
1.
2.
3.
4.

F. Neighborhood Improvement
1.
2.
3.
4.

C. Recreational or Social
1.
2.
3.
4.

G. Social Action/Civil Rights
1.
2.
3.
4.

D. Political
1.
2.
3.
4.

H. Business, Professional or Work Ass'n
1.
2.
3.
4.

#66
This question has to do with the kinds of things people in this household do when they are not working. You may indicate who in the household does it — you, another adult or children (if applicable), and how often the activity is engaged in.

Person in the household who engages in the activity (check)	Activity	Frequency (check)
	Vacation trips	
	Attend professional athletic games	
	Attend large dances in clubs or in ballrooms	
	Attend house parties at others' homes	
	Attend large conventions	
	Read books for pleasure	
	Sit and talk with family member	
	Sit and talk with friends	
	Play cards	
	Go to the movies	
	Invite people over for dinner	
	Invite people over for a house party	
	Go to dinner in a restaurant	
	Go to dinner in the home of a relative or friend	
	Go bowling	
	Play tennis	
	Go swimming	
	Read newspaper	
	Watch TV	
	Listen to the radio	

#66 (continued)

Person in the household
who engages in the
activity (check)

Frequency (check)

Activity

Attend club meetings
Fix up the house
Repair car
Garden
Sewing or knitting
Go shopping
Go to concerts
Go to lectures
Visit museum
Jog or walk
Fish or hunt
Camping
Do volunteer work in the community
Do volunteer work at the church or synagogue
Do volunteer work at the school
Go to school and study
Other (specify)

#67
What were the happy times that the members of this household have shared during recent years?
When were they and what was done?

#68
What were the sad times that the members of this household have shared during recent years?
When were they and what was done?

#69
If you were to sum it up, what would you say this household is trying to accomplish in life?

#70
Have you accomplished this?

#71
If not, what have been the barriers to this accomplishment?

INDEX